PIANO PRACTICE FOR THE ADVANCING STUDENT

Continuing the Journey Begun in
"Handbook for Piano Practice"

ALSO BY VICTORIA B. STEARNS

Handbook for Piano Practice

PIANO PRACTICE FOR THE ADVANCING STUDENT

Continuing the Journey Begun in
"Handbook for Piano Practice"

For Students and Teachers

Victoria B. Stearns

W. R. PARKS
www.WRParks.com

Dedication:
for Elaine Jenning
and all fellow travelers on the piano journey

Copyright © 2018 by Victoria B. Stearns

ISBN: 978-0-88493-046-4

Library of Congress Control Number: 2018963609

Published by William R. Parks *www.wrparks.com*

There is no end to learning

Robert Schumann, *House Rules and Maxims for Young Musicians*

The House Rules and Maxims for Young Musicians (also translated as *Aphorisms*, or *Advice to Young Musicians*) a list of remarkably pithy and helpful statements, apply to older musicians as well, to maintain an attitude of always learning something new, much in the spirit of Thomas Jefferson's often quoted remark about age: "though an old man, I am a young gardener." There are many translations of this work available online, and also in print (Robert Schumann, *Advice to Young Musicians*, Henry Hugo Pierson, translator, which includes the original German; *On Music and Musicians*, Robert Schumann, edited by Konrad Wolff, Paul Rosenfeld, translator). I have tried to select the best translation of each individual quote based on the original German. There is a new book*, Robert Schumann's Advice to Young Musicians, revisited by* Steven Isserlis (London: Faber and Faber, 2016) which presents an updated version for modern readers.

Some of Schumann's aphorisms will appear in the text of this book; they will be italicized.

CONTENTS

INTRODUCTION: THE JOURNEY CONTINUES 9

OVERVIEW AND REVIEW 11
- How much you already know
- Assessment checklist
- Troubleshooting immediate issues
- Honing your skills
- Your own goals
- How much to practice
- Your instrument and its maintenance
- Lessons: scheduling, assignments
- Sight reading and playing music without practicing
- THE CANON
- Introduction and bibliography
- Eras before the piano: Renaissance and early Baroque
- Theme and Variations
- BACH
- Other Baroque Masters
- Ornamentation
- HAYDN
- MOZART
- BEETHOVEN
- Review of the Classic period style
- SCHUBERT
- SCHUMANN
- CHOPIN
- Other early nineteenth century masters
- Playing in the Romantic style
- The Pedal
- BRAHMS
- The Golden Age of the Piano
- DEBUSSY
- Impressionism and French Composers after Debussy
- BARTÓK
- The Twentieth Century

MAKING MUSIC COME ALIVE 83
- What is the composer trying to say?
- The professional sound
- Why does a piece "fall apart"?
- Improving your playing: building dexterity, troubleshooting
- Scales, Cadences, Arpeggios
- Christmas Carols
- Pointers for Style: a summary
- Works requiring musical maturity

POP AND JAZZ 100
- Music everyone should know

PLAYING FOR AND WITH OTHERS 105
- Memorizing
- Concert dress and etiquette
- Preparing for auditions
- Playing chamber music and accompanying
- Community service

CONTINUING THE JOURNEY: MUSIC FOR A LIFETIME 109
Composers who did not write piano music, or who wrote very little
A few novels with musical themes and miscellaneous readings
Final thoughts and some general suggestions

INTRODUCTION: THE JOURNEY CONTINUES

"There are few worthwhile skills that can be achieved without a good deal of effort expended over a long period of time." Wise advice from His Holiness the Dalai Lama, which is an explanation for my use of the word "journey".

Welcome aboard! Those who have traveled this far in learning the piano have been "bitten by the music bug" for lack of a better description. You want music to be part of your life, and thus it will be. You are over the hump, the major hurdle, and you are now able to play some original piano music. With a bit more careful practice, you will be able to play a great deal more. Music is cumulative, like mathematics; it builds on a solid foundation, which once learned well, you never forget; you haven't forgotten how to add and subtract. You are joining students from all the ages in the time-honored tradition of the study of music, considered extremely important in ancient Greece and in the Middle Ages, and which should be viewed in the same manner today.

At this point, it is a good idea to take stock, so to speak, to assess strengths and find any weaknesses to be addressed. Your goals are a very important consideration: do you need to prepare for college or conservatory admission, including auditions; do you hope to get a job accompanying an individual or a group, like a church choir? Do you wish to do community service? Is there a special area of interest that needs extra time? A favorite composer? Simply to play and enjoy?

What I term the "balanced musical diet" will stand you in good stead: learning works from all the main eras of music history will build a solid background. This forms the scope of this book, which begins where the previous one (*Handbook for Piano Practice*) ended. It will serve as a guide to and through much of the more advanced literature, up to becoming a music major and beginning a musical career. It is not necessary to read it entirely through from the first page; reading the sections pertinent to your current work will be useful. The purpose of the book is to inform and encourage, always emphasizing getting the most out of your time spent practicing.

Keep in mind that classical music (using the word in its broadest terms) is enjoyed daily by music lovers, which makes music stand apart from literature or even art. How many people are reading 17th century poetry, 18th century novels, or looking at the art of those centuries on a daily basis? By playing music, you are making a *connection* with the greatest composers. You are at the threshold of a vast treasure trove, and the door is unlocked.

Are you changing teachers? This occurs for many reasons. Some teachers only give lessons to a certain level, or because of a move, a new school. The new teacher can appraise your skills in terms of strengths and weaknesses. Your old teacher can also do this. This is a good time to evaluate and take steps to strengthen and improve.

Will you be adding any additional activities to your schedule? Are you learning a second instrument, singing in a choir, taking on a job, or changing jobs, participating in new activities (exercise, sports, social groups, volunteering) all of which take away time from the piano.

Is it time for a new piano? You will need a firm action to reap the most benefits from your practice. If you foresee a possible purchase in the future, check out the local music stores, ask your tuner for advice. Often there are sales of stock purchased from another location (such as another music store); however, you do not want a piano that has had heavy use, such as one from a music school. I have known people who have purchased Steinways for rock-bottom prices at estate sales. If someone is selling a piano privately, it is worth the investment to pay your piano tuner to appraise it. A better piano will yield better results, and you will enjoy your practice a great deal more.

A note regarding printed music and books:
In this transitional age of the Internet, there are constant changes, sometimes at dizzying speed. Some musicians now use electronic reading devices. Some older books are reissued (a caveat here) with entirely different titles. Short articles, and even full texts, are sometimes available online. The book you are looking for (with an outrageous price for a used copy) may be reissued in the future, or found at a book or yard sale. Articles, even full texts, appear online, and much music can be downloaded for free.

OVERVIEW AND REVIEW (This is not a test)

To repeat, this is not a test: it is to demonstrate how much you have already been exposed to, how much you have learned, how much you might be expected to know, and how to find the answers. All the basics are covered, certainly the lion's share of piano knowledge. There are some more terms and techniques that occur in advancing studies, which will be covered subsequently.

You need *not* memorize these terms, as the ones that occur most frequently will become part of your musical knowledge, automatically through repetition. Once learned, you will remember.

A good way to check your understanding is to think about how you would explain it or teach it to someone else. If you do not already own a music dictionary, now is the time to acquire one. It will be more useful than the Internet, and actually quicker. Two good choices are *Essential Dictionary of Music* by L. C. Harnsberger (Alfred Publications) and *The Harvard Concise Dictionary of Music and Musicians* by Don Michael Randel. Aspiring music majors should eventually own *The Harvard Dictionary of Music*.

Teachers can use this as an evaluation, what needs more work, study, or information, and for finding strengths and weaknesses.

Learn the fundamental laws of harmony.
Do not be afraid of the words "theory, thorough-bass, counterpoint," they will meet you halfway if you do the same.
R.S.
Schumann's comments can be expanded to include all the basics of the language of music, just as you learn vocabulary and grammar when you study a language.

NOTE READING

PITCH and GRAND STAFF
Treble and bass clefs (write these out as well as identifying them)
Notes on the staff for each clef
Leger lines
8va, 8va bassa, 15va

Sharps, double sharps
Flats, double flats
Naturals
Accidentals (rules for individual measure and individual clef)

KEY SIGNATURES (how many can you identify? and write out)
Change of key signature within a composition

Repeat sign
Da capo al fine
Dal segno al fine
First and second endings
Coda

RHYTHM

Time or meter signature (explain the principle of the top and bottom number)

$\frac{2}{4}$ $\frac{3}{4}$ $\frac{4}{4}$ $\frac{5}{4}$ $\frac{3}{8}$ $\frac{6}{8}$ $\frac{9}{8}$ $\frac{12}{8}$

Difference between $\frac{3}{4}$ and $\frac{6}{8}$

Which meter has two "large" beats per bar? Which has only one?
What is the meter for a waltz? A minuet? A march?

Common time $\frac{4}{4}$ (what is the symbol?)

Cut time (alla breve) $\frac{2}{2}$ (what is the symbol?)

Values of notes and their rests (write these out)
Whole
(note that a whole rest is used for a silent bar, no matter what the meter)
Half
Quarter
Eighth
Sixteenth
Thirty-second
Sixty-fourth

Use of the beam to connect certain notes, and the use of "flags" for the same notes.
Note that flags are always used in vocal music.

Dotted notes: make sure that you understand the principle.
There will even be double-dotted notes in advanced work, but infrequently.
Triplets
Duplets

Tied notes (and how to tell if a note is tied or not: difference between a tie and a slur)
Change of meter signature within the composition

SCALES AND KEYS
Definition of a scale, and how to find the key signature
Circle of Fifths (explain, and how much can you fill in?)
How many scales have you learned?
What are the enharmonic scales (do you understand the principle?)
F sharp and G flat, B and C flat, D flat and C sharp

Can you play a five-finger exercise in all 12 major keys and all 12 minor keys? If you can, you can play the triad as well.

Pattern for major scales (write out)

How to find the relative minor, and the relative major from the minor)
What is the tonic minor (extra credit)

Patterns for the minor scales
Three forms: natural, harmonic, and melodic

Other scales
Chromatic
Whole tone
Pentatonic
Modes (you have probably encountered some without realizing it, such as the Dorian)

Cadences and simple progressions (can you play these?)

SCALE BOOK. If you don't already own one, now is the time to get one.

ARTICULATION AND PHRASING
Look up the definitions and the correct way to indicate these:

staccato
      How hot is this potato? Varying degrees of staccato, including markings for mezzo staccato, staccatissimo, and the old staccato markings found in some editions.

legato (slur)
      Can be short or long, a phrase marking on a few notes or the whole "musical sentence" itself. Difference between legato and a tie.

tenuto
marcato
accents
forzando
rinforzando
sforzando

Definition of a phrase, a theme and a motif (look these up)

DYNAMICS AND EXPRESSION
Take note of all the Italian words you have learned

piano, pianissimo, pianississimo
forte, fortissimo, fortississimo
fortepiano
mezzo (combined with another word)
subito
molto and poco, poco a poco
Definition, abbreviation, and symbol for
crescendo, decrescendo, diminuendo

TEMPO AND TEMPERAMENT
Here is a basic grid from slowest to fastest:
largo, lento, adagio, andante, allegretto, allegro, presto

Some variants: prestissimo, larghetto, andantino (note there are two definitions of this). Other common tempi: vivace, moderato, scherzando, con brio.

Increasing tempo: più mosso, accelerando, stringendo, stretto
Decreasing tempo: meno mosso, ritardando, ritenuto, slentando, allargando, calando, perdendosi, morendo, smorzando, mancando
Sustained tempo: sostenuto

Symbols for caesura and fermata, with definitions
Definitions of rubato, a piacere, a tempo, l'istesso tempo, segue, attacca

Some more descriptive words:
affetuoso, agitato, amabile, animato, appassionato, cantabile, dolce, espressivo, con fuoco, giocoso, grave, grazioso, leggier, maestoso, mesto, pesante, scherzando

Some more basic (musical) Italian:
ma, non, più (mosso), col, con (con moto), meno, mezzo, poco, molto, assai, tanto, troppo (ma non troppo), subito, ossia, quasi, sempre, senza, sopra, sotto (sotto voce), primo and secondo (in piano duets)

Going forward: Italian was originally considered to be the language of music, but by the nineteenth century, many composers began using terms in their own language, perhaps to be more precise or descriptive. There will be musical terms in French and German to look up, and you want the real meaning of the word, not a translation into Italian (*bewegt* conveys more meaning than allegro), and you will think in a different way about the work you are studying. You can look up definitions online, but it is much better to have a music dictionary handy.

ORNAMENTS ("grace notes") and other special effects: My advice is, do not be overly concerned about these until you encounter them, and then your teacher will guide you. A good edition with explanations (called "realizations") will speed you on your way, and later on, you will "feel" what sounds right. The best way to practice is to go through the work at least once without ornamentation, so you can find out the importance of the main note that has the ornament attached to it. Here again, a music dictionary is a great help with the definitions and symbols.

How many of these do you know, including the symbols (look up on a chart of ornaments)

acciaccatura
appoggiatura (short and long)
mordent
inverted mordent
trills (above and below)
arpeggiated ("broken") chord
glissando
tremolo
turn

crossed hands
m.d., m.g., m.s.

what is an Alberti bass? (extra credit)

pedals (identify the three)

tre corde ("damper" or "loud" sometimes called sostenuto)
middle (sostenuto) not on all pianos
una corde ("soft")

THEORY
half step
whole step
intervals
    major, minor, perfect
chords
what is a triad?
    major and minor triads
inversions of triads
augmented triads
diminished triads
scales and key signatures (*yes, again*)
circle of 5ths
relative and tonic minors
Picardy third (extra credit)
triads on the degrees (steps) of the scale
primary triads
cadences
simple chord progression
seventh chords
    dominant seventh
    full diminished seventh
note and chord "spelling": (understanding of enharmonics)
    this can be as simple as understanding why F sharp is not G flat, even though they are the same key on the keyboard
pedal point (extra credit)
overtone series (not necessary to learn, but to understand the underlying principles)

FORMS
sonata-allegro form
what is a sonatina?
movements of a sonata (what does movement mean?)
ABA form (what do the letters signify?)
minuet and trio (what does trio mean in this context?)

scherzo
rondo
theme and variations (extra credit)
dance movements (e.g., in a suite)
suite
prelude
etude

what is a melody with accompaniment and how does it differ from contrapuntal writing (counterpoint)
what is counterpoint? what does the word "voice" mean?
what is a round or canon?
what is going on in a two-part invention? a three-part invention?
what is a fugue? (extra credit)
can you explain the following:
- timbre
- tone color
- equal temperament
- modulation
- chamber music vs. orchestral music

This previous section is not meant to be overwhelming, merely a long view of the possibilities, and to be used for reference in remedying any weak spots. The following section likewise is not designed to discourage: learning about composers and the various periods of style casts a piano piece in a new light: part of the vast musical repertoire and opens the door to more music appreciation. By learning a piece by Mozart or Beethoven, for example, you now have a perspective from which to build more knowledge, when you hear one of their symphonies or chamber works.

A Mini-History of Musical Eras, with emphasis on the piano

MEDIEVAL
Monophonic (one voice at a time) with Gregorian chant as the prime example.
Then think about a canon (round) where additional voices are added: now you have polyphony, more than one voice.

RENAISSANCE

Now there is more complex polyphony, and more instruments to play it. Dance music (pavane, gaillarde) played by instruments, including the virginals (precursor of keyboard instruments). Vocal music includes madrigals (secular) and motets and Masses for sacred music. The Golden Age of English music occurs during the Elizabethan age.

BAROQUE (Bach, Handel, Scarlatti)

The well-tempered tuning (equal half steps of the scale) expands the possibilities for composition, along with the newer forms: prelude and fugue, toccata, suite of dances, sonata da chiesa, sonata da camera, concerto grosso. The piano makes its appearance in this period, but does not replace the harpsichord as yet.

CLASSIC (Haydn, Mozart, Beethoven)

Classic sonata form dominates this period, in instrumental sonatas, concertos, chamber works, and symphonies. The piano replaces the harpsichord, but still does not have a very strong sound. Sonata form is first movement form, and there are usually three or four movements to a major work, with the second movement slow, the third a minuet and trio ("upgraded" to a scherzo, by Beethoven) and the final movement a fast tempo, such as allegro or presto. Most works of this period follow this basic plan, though there will be exceptions.

ROMANTIC (Schumann, Chopin, Brahms)

This is the "golden age" of the piano, as it becomes a much more powerful instrument with an expanded range. Composers now extend the possibilities of sonata form, and begin writing the "character piece" for piano, with a descriptive title, along with the new forms such as the nocturne, concert etude, ballade, album leaf, songs without words, waltz, impromptu, rhapsody, intermezzo, capriccio.
Orchestras are now larger, with many more instruments, and the works they now can play have a more spectacular orchestration.

IMPRESSIONISM (Debussy, Ravel)
This is a musical period most closely related to the art movement at the time, with titled compositions, describing the moment, a sense of immediacy, mood evoking harmonies, expanded use of the pedal.

TWENTIETH CENTURY (Bartók, Prokofiev, Stravinsky, Copland, Schoenberg).
The long heyday of the piano is fading fast, but has not disappeared entirely. Most composers are now writing larger works for larger musical forces. Many styles are present, from atonality to neoclassicism and minimalism. There is the influence of jazz.

Why do you need to comprehend all this? The more musical knowledge you have, the more motivation you will have to keep learning and exploring, discovering music new to you (including "non-piano" music). Learning will become easier, and you will play more musically as things begin to make more sense, with theory (what is going on here?) and stylistically. Knowing what key you are in, for instances, orients you to where you are ("you are here" on a map of a gallery) a kind of musical geography. Being aware of the stylistic period of the composer will give you guidelines to proper interpretation, and gives you the historical timeline. All of which enhance your musical life.

Bear in mind that in games and sports you have to learn the rules and play by them. With only a vague idea of how a sport is played, you don't have much appreciation as a spectator.

Any time that music practice seems overwhelming might be a good time to read this passage by Carl Demler, quoted by Perri Knize in *Grand Obsession* (p.166):
"Music is the closest link to the inner world, the higher worlds. Playing music is a self-transforming experience. The experience of being a conduit for the spirit of the composer, who is also a conduit for the divine. It's the divine that is in all of us. Music transforms. When it is played, emanations come from that music. This is the secret influence of music throughout the ages. It could have a healing effect on illnesses, illness from having the wrong vibration in your body."
You can open the door and have a direct connection with the greatest masters of music.

ASSESSMENT CHECKLIST

(Teachers could use this perhaps once a year without telling the student, merely for guidelines for what should be emphasized and what materials to choose)

PRACTICE HABITS
Does the student aim to practice every day, for a set amount of time? Is there a specific time of day, for an easier transition into making the playing of music a part of the person's life (more on practice later).

REPERTOIRE
Not many remember to do this, but it is useful to keep a list (notebook) of works learned, or at least checked off in the tables of contents.

Which of the following have already been learned?
Bach, Short Preludes
Bach, Two-Part Inventions
Haydn, Sonata in C, H35 (L48)
Mozart, Sonata in C, K 545, Sonata in B-flat K570
Beethoven, Sonatas Op. 49, nos. 1 and 2
What 19th and 20th century works?
Sight reading skills

SCALES. How many have been learned, for how many octaves, hands together?
How many arpeggios and basic chords?

THEORY. Key signatures, basic chords in each key, Circle of Fifths.

NOTE READING.
Problems with either clef, or changing clefs.
Leger lines, accidentals, key signatures
Too much learning by rote, looking at hands instead of the music

RHYTHM PROBLEMS.
Does the student have a good grasp of the steady beat, or an erratic sense of rhythm and tempo? Is there rushing or slowing down? In every piece, or in just a particularly tricky one? Does the student know how to

figure out where the beats are? Is there a preferred method of counting (aloud, foot or toe-tapping?)

INTERPRETATION.
Does the student have a sense of the style of the work being played? Is the student *listening* to the sounds being made? The two extremes are the mechanical player and the overenthusiastic, gung-ho player who overemotes, usually keeping a foot constantly on the pedal, and neither one is actually listening. What pieces has the student enjoyed, or done especially well? A particular composer, pieces that are slow and melodic, or fast and zippy?

Special strengths: *what is the student best at?*

POSSIBLE REMEDIES AND TROUBLESHOOTING: a few suggestions

Recheck posture and seating, as well as hand position. Adjustments may be necessary, even for a different piece of music. Make sure the music is centered on the music stand. Do you have any stiffness, aches or pains? Concentrating too hard that you tense up and get stiff? Shoulder rolls can help, and try taking a break every 45 minutes, even just to stand up and stretch.
Instead of thinking of straightening your back military fashion, from the top down, thrusting the shoulders back, try this: think upwards from the base of the spine, and you will have good posture, but not stiff. Relax your shoulders below your ears. Students under the age of thirty most likely won't have problems, unless they are tensing up or sitting in an awkward position, but should try to form good habits now, to avoid problems in the future. You want your spine and lower back to be strong.

Do you need eyeglasses or a change of prescription if you already wear them? Many people (including those who work at computers all day) need special glasses just for the computer or piano. I have seen such glasses termed "piano glasses" at the optician's. More lighting may also be needed; try more and see if this makes a difference.

Try a short regiment of scales, arpeggios, and exercises, to determine if you are using too much arm motion. Too much arm motion is unnecessary and tiring: in scale-like passages, try to tuck the thumb under without moving the arm. Recheck your hand position also, and make sure you have your hands close to the keyboard so you can press into the keys easily.

Take good care of your hands, and this means more than manicuring. Nails should be kept short, if you want to maximize the possibilities of your technique. You should be able to feel a finger tip, not a fingernail, on the key. Practice safe habits when using tools (e.g., scissors, knives, trowels, pruners, hammers) and always use caution. Wear gloves for such jobs as gardening and cleaning woodwork. Have some really warm mittens if you live in a cold climate, and if it gets bitterly cold, put on a light pair of gloves underneath.

READING THE NOTES ACCURATELY

For issues with note reading and key signatures, the answer is to WRITE THEM OUT on music paper. At this point, the student should have a music manuscript notebook (staff paper). If you can't make a G clef, sit for about 10 minutes practicing them and then you will be able. Some people like flash cards, but they only help if you use them, and they are better when you make them yourself. For some reason, students seem to resist the actual writing, but this is the best way to learn. When you learn a foreign language, you have to translate both ways, and write things out. The well-known mnemonic devices can help, and so can looking up the notes on a reference sheet that you have made yourself. Recognizing octaves as well as the other intervals by their "shape" (theory, again) will help in note reading. Read either top down or bottom up from the note you recognize for sure. Learn to count up or down for the leger lines from a note you know. Think of <u>accidentals</u> as *a red flag* for that measure only, and learn to make a quick scan to see if that particular note recurs within the same bar.

RHYTHM PROBLEMS.

Pianists unfortunately have more rhythm problems than instrumentalists, who have the benefit of playing with others, sometimes even under a conductor. The basic idea is to FEEL the beat, once you figure out how many there are per measure. Sight reading, learning folk songs or other simple pieces, and analyzing the meter (3/4 for a waltz, for instance) may help. For complex measures, <u>doubling the time</u> (i.e., counting eight beats in 4/4 time) will help to figure out the rhythm Be aware of the various meter signatures, and try to relate them to a work you know. Work out about two bars at a time before going on. In order to "feel" the beat, you have to do something to "feel" it, such as beating your foot, tapping your toe, beating with one hand while practicing the other. Counting aloud works for some, but not many. For difficult measures, mark the beats in with a pencil line (you needn't be concerned about what number beat it is, only that the measure totals correctly) and in some cases, you even work backwards. Get out those anthologies of easier pieces and go through them from a rhythmic standpoint (march, minuet, gigue, etc.) If you put a heavy accent on the strong beats (totally unmusical, but if you realize you are doing this, it is easy to remove later) it may help to figure out the measure.

LACK OF FLEXIBILITY AND DEXTERITY
Recheck posture and seated location. Practicing more scales, arpeggios and exercises should help. These needn't be burdensome: set a timer and see how much you can accomplish in five minutes, ten minutes. Try practicing exercises at a separate time from your main practice. Notice if you have too much arm movement.
<u>More on scales</u>. The goal is four octaves, hands together. How many do you know? A good one to review is E major, in contrary motion. You could work out a plan with your teacher, for instance, one scale per month, which would be twelve in a year. If you have an audition deadline, you could adjust that plan. Make sure you understand how the Circle of Fifths works. Can you write out all the key signatures? Can you identify and play the tonic chord, its inversions and arpeggios? Also, be sure that you realize that the fingering for many scales is the same, so that you aren't doing any unnecessary work. Scales are necessary for good technique, dexterity, flexibility, finger strength, and

memory. You want to learn the fingering well, with a firm pressing into the keys, at a *moderate* speed. Exercises and scales played at high speed are a waste of time.

Learn hands separately, and go slowly when combining your hands. If the hands confuse each other, go back to hands separately. Recheck your hand position. The slightest adjustment may make quite a difference (you want to be able to reach the black keys easily). Try hands in contrary motion (especially for scales that finger like C) and hands two octaves apart. Notice where the thumbs fall. Mark the scales you have learned on a Circle of Fifths. Do a periodic review of the scales you have learned. You might try to do them by fingering "family" or by key signatures, major and minor (tonic or relative), or chromatically. (See the chapter on Scales)

Arpeggios. Learn a simpler pattern first, before tackling the standard version (in the scale books). Check your left hand fingering, and consult your teacher if the given fingering seems awkward; there are variations you can use. Again, practice hands separately.

WHAT IS LEFT TO LEARN?
We should return to Robert Schumann's advice on page 5. All the previous material, I hope, is not too overwhelming. You have already had the largest portion of musical terms and an introduction to theory. A C scale will always be a C scale, as a C triad is always a C triad. This knowledge will stay with you. There will be some musical terms you won't remember, but can always look up. French and German terms will appear, along with rubato, more pedaling techniques, and a few "special effects" such as glissando, which is actually quite rare. There will be more complex rhythms, such as two against three, three against four, but with efficient practice, should not present much of a problem. There will be more complex harmony, but you do not have to learn how to analyze your pieces unless you want to, or are working on a college assignment. These remarks cover piano music up to the beginning of the twentieth century. The main issues now will be strengthening your technique, endurance, and refining your style of playing. This is also a time for an assessment of your goals, with your age a consideration. Are you working towards a musical career, or do you simply want a solid background, for a life-long interest in learning more music as a

serious avocation? If you have any special interests (favorite composer, a piece you really want to learn, pop music) make sure your teacher is aware of this.

Purchasing music. Complete editions are generally always more economical and inherently more useful, as you have all the sonatas in one place, for future study as well as the present. Which edition? Your teacher's choice will guide you, as well as checking editions in a library. Online resources (IMPetrucci for free downloads, Amazon and SheetMusicPlus for purchases), used book sales; all are sources at the present time. Some good editions go out of print, but you might be able to acquire a used copy. Publishers do reissue editions, and Dover Publications concentrates most of its offerings on reprints. The student should have a large size music manuscript notebook, and a folder or binder for handouts and printouts. Some sort of organizational system is advisable, if the teacher gives out many loose pages. Exercise books that are useful include those by Hanon and Pischna (*The Little Pischna*, for starters). There is an interesting modernization of Hanon entitled *Hanon Revisited*, by Arthur Gold and Robert Fizdale, the late duo-piano team. They are the only musicians I know of who have written a cookbook, titled with their names, which incidentally is an interesting volume with good anecdotes as well as recipes. Eventually you will want to add the *51 Exercises* by Johannes Brahms, which may appear very intimidating at first, but selections can be (and usually are) made from them, and they are extremely lovely sounding, absolutely musical, in spite of the fact that they are exercises.

How many lessons? The goal is one lesson per week, approximately one hour, at this stage. The ideal number of lessons per year would be around 48 (remember this is the "ideal" number). Forty lessons are good, but if you drop to around 30, progress will not be as smooth. More advanced students, who can work well independently, can do with fewer lessons.

How much to practice? A certain number of years of practice is necessary to reach certain levels of competence, a fact known to the music world for decades, and only recently explained by Malcolm Gladwell (*The Outliers*). If you don't have the concert stage as your goal, you needn't be concerned about the 10,000 hours needed for mastery. However, every hour, in order to "count" towards the goal, has to be efficient practice. You can crunch some numbers if you are interested. Oscar Peterson reportedly practiced 12 hours a day, which means he attained the goal in less than three years. (*and* then some: listen to his playing to hear someone absolutely creative and totally involved in music)

The best way to practice is to increase the time *gradually*, so it becomes an integral part of your life that you *want* to do, and not regard it as a chore. The same time each day usually helps, but is not always possible. When you no longer have to ask the question, *How much should I practice?* you are already well on your journey.

The key strategy, which has been stated before, is *efficient practice*, to get the most from your time spent, explained in detail in the *Handbook for Piano Practice.* You want some time for technique (exercises and scales, but you don't have to do these every day) time to work on the difficult passages of the pieces you are studying, going over those many times rather than repeating the parts you already know well over and over again. Make sure you take breaks, and definitely do some stretches after 45 minutes. Include some sight reading as often as possible, to keep your skills sharp. You want to be looking at something "new" all the time, and find out that there are many things you can play without any practice at all! Sight reading and going through pieces on the "review list" should be done weekly, if at all possible.

If you have a "block", meaning a piece isn't going well at all, try something else. If that doesn't work, leave the piano and do something else entirely. Sometimes it's even a good idea to let a work "simmer" (especially if you have worked on it for some time) while you learn something new. If too many pieces are abandoned, or unfinished, it's time to take a look at the choices. Too difficult? Student doesn't like the composer? Too many pieces on the student's workload? In general, three works, such as a prelude and fugue by Bach, a Beethoven sonata, and one other piece, are ample. For some people with busy schedules, way too much. It's important to look for a variety of musical styles, so balancing this "diet" may be more difficult with fewer choices. The student should be advised to explore within the music already in hand, to look at other works by the same composer, and other works in general, such as in anthologies. It is surprising to find that hardly any students do this.

For a good sense of progress, several shorter works might replace one long one, and even some "easier" pieces, which add to the student's repertoire, sense of accomplishment, and musical style. If you learn only one piece by a composer, it might not even be particularly "typical" of the composer's style, and you might not like the piece, which will discourage you from learning any more by that composer, or even listening to the composer's other works. At least three pieces by any composer should be learned, just for starters.

If a student has a specific goal, such as a college admission, the requirements should be known at least two years in advance of any auditions, so there is ample time for choice and for learning.

THE CANON

You must gradually learn to know all the important works of all the important masters.
Spiritual, like bodily nourishment, must be simple and solid. The masters have provided it.
R.S.

It is indeed a daunting, formidable task to attempt to list the greatest composers for piano. I approach this endeavor with both trepidation and respect, and emphasize this clarification: this information is to serve merely as an introduction to the highlights and essential works, not an exhaustive list. No presumption is intended, just to provide a pointer to the important works, opening the door, so to speak, much as a travel guide lists the major sights. Not everything can be included, and many composers unfortunately will not be found here (check the lists in the recommended books) as you don't want to limit yourself to the composers here. Different material will be needed from time to time, much as you couldn't eat a "great" meal cooked by a master chef every day and continue to appreciate it.

Along with the commentary, you will occasionally find books or references to the composer's piano works. These are not requirements; they are included only for a sense to completeness, where to search for more information. *The New Grove's Dictionary of Music and Musicians* (also online) provides extensive biographical information on composers, including the listings of a composer's complete works, and much bibliography if you want to find a biography of a composer. There is so much information now online that it almost seems redundant to list references, but be advised that there is much misinformation online, and some downright errors.

Sometimes people get off on a tangent, for example, searching for the "real cause" of Mozart's demise, or the true "immortal beloved" of Beethoven. Such pursuits are non-essential and unsolvable, plus they take time away from practicing, where it would be much better spent. You needn't read lengthy biographies, but it is always useful to know a little about the composer's life, circumstances for the writing of a certain work, and your understanding increases as you learn more about the "temper of the times" (*Zeitgeist*, if you'd like the fancier word). Why are there so many minuets, for instance? To repeat, please do remember that it is far more important to *play* the music rather than dwell on the misfortunes of the composer. So many had difficult lives, serious health problems, died untimely deaths, but the bottom line remains: *they left a legacy of great music*.

Bear in mind that you should learn three or four pieces by a composer before making any immediate decisions about how you like the music. Some pieces will naturally not be your cup of tea, at least at the present time (try rediscovering some of these pieces years later, you may be surprised). Heed your teacher's advice if you are attempting to tackle a long, difficult work before you are ready. It is usually more beneficial to learn several shorter works to get a grasp of the compositional style.

How to make a list of the "best" or "greatest" composers? Different people will make different lists. Beethoven usually wins the popularity contests, whether the voters are the listening audiences or professional musicians. Anthony Tommasini, the chief music critic of *The New York Times*, wrote several articles about this, and eventually revealed his list of ten (you can read this online). Verdi and Wagner are on his list, but excluded here because they wrote so little for piano, and are known as opera composers. I am also including a list of composers who did not write much (or anything) for the piano, with a few suggestions for works to explore.

What constitutes the canon of piano music? Most pianists would reply, the 48 and the 32, meaning *The Well-Tempered Clavier* of J. S. Bach, and the *Piano Sonatas* of Ludwig van Beethoven. This book will have detailed chapters on the main masters, information on the other masters of each stylistic period, arranged chronologically, up to the early twentieth century, with suggestions for what works to study *first*, which ones are the most "approachable" or "doable", as so many works are too difficult or daunting. This is a guide for practice, with stylistic hints, the basic works, what forms to expect, works not to be missed, works to get you on your way. Every great composer has certain hallmarks of style, individual characteristics, such as compositional devices, use of harmony and rhythmic patterns, which enable you to recognize that composer, but these are not always readily apparent in every piece, and not in the first time listening or playing.

As stated previously, it is beyond the scope of this book to provide an exhaustive list of piano literature. Here are some good sources of information:

The first two titles give lists of repertoire with brief commentary:

Friskin, James, and Irwin Freundlich. *Music for Piano*. New York, Holt, Rinehart and Winston, 1954. Reissued by Dover Publications. This volume is arranged chronologically, and is out of date regarding the second half of the twentieth century, but is a trove of valuable information by two teachers at Juilliard. I will refer to it in the text as F&F.

Hinson, Maurice. *Guide to the Pianist's Repertoire*. 3d edition. Bloomington, Indiana University Press, 1987. Arranged alphabetically, and now in a 4th edition (keep a watch for further updating)

The following books discuss piano literature in depth. Some have been out of print (look for reissues, with a possible change of title). Most do not evaluate the difficulty of the work being discussed from the student's point of view.

Apel, Willi. *Masters of the Keyboard*. Cambridge, MA, Harvard University Press, 1952.

Ferguson, Donald N. *Piano Music of Six Great Composers*. New York, Prentice-Hall, 1947. Some of the easier literature of each master is suggested here. The composers selected are Beethoven, Schubert, Schumann, Chopin, Brahms, and Debussy (the author is cleaving strictly to the term "piano")

Gillespie, John. *Five Centuries of Keyboard Music*. Belmont, CA, Wadsworth Publishing Co., 1965. (reissued by Dover Publications). A wealth of information.

Gordon, Stewart. *A History of Keyboard Literature*. New York: Schirmer, 1996.
Extremely thorough and extremely expensive.

Hutcheson, Ernest. *The Literature of the Piano*. New York, Knopf, 1948. A revised edition by Rudolf Ganz was issued in 1964. Much valuable information, and extremely useful tips, but can seem outdated with mention of concert artists who are now unfamiliar.

Kirby, F. E. *A Short History of Keyboard Music*. New York: The Free Press, 1966.
An expanded edition, *Music for Piano*, issued in 2003.

Mathews, Denis, ed. *Keyboard Music*. Harmondsworth, Penguin Books, 1972.
Covers all the stylistic periods with chapters by authoritative writers.

Rowland, David, ed. *The Cambridge Companion to the Piano*. Cambridge, Cambridge University Press, 1998. The second half of the book is devoted to piano repertoire.

Alfred Publishing has issued three volumes by Willard A. Palmer and Margery Halford, (*Introduction to*) *The Baroque Era*, *The Classical Era*, and *The Romantic Era*. All three have excellent introductions to the style, detailed explanations of ornamentation, and much additional information regarding the selected works (all of an intermediate level). I wish all the commentary could be printed in a combined volume, along with all the biographical information about the composers that is included in the Alfred publications.

THE ERAS BEFORE THE PIANO: RENAISSANCE AND EARLY BAROQUE

There is an extensive treasure trove of material from these times, largely ignored, probably because there is so much actual literature written for the piano that keeps people busy. There are some issues regarding ornamentation, but there are more editions now that give explanations. A few pieces actually do "work" better on the harpsichord, are not so effective on the piano, but there is still much useful material to explore. An accessible way to approach this era would be to look for an anthology of early keyboard music. Listen very carefully to the sound, as this is a time before well-tempered tuning. You might find it "quaint" and like it very much. Search out some recordings by instrumental groups.

ENGLAND. The Elizabethan Age, termed the "golden age" had great keyboard composers as well as writers. William Byrd, John Bull, and Orlando Gibbons are the trio of music masters. The main collections of their works are *Parthenia* (published in 1612-13, and edited for today's musicians by Thurston Dart; this collection was the first printed keyboard music in England) and the *Fitzwilliam Virginal Book* (two volumes, edited by J. A. Fuller Maitland and W. Barclay Squire) which include works by other composers as well. There are volumes of selections from the two volumes. There is an additional collection of William Byrd's works entitled *My Ladye Nevells Booke of Virginal Music*. *Anne Cromwell's Virginal Book (*1638) edited by Howard Ferguson, contains additional pieces, mainly anonymous, while *Elizabeth Rogers Hir Virginal Booke* (1656) edited by Charles J.F. Cofone, contains pieces by many composers (although they appear anonymously) is described as one of the last collections of virginal music. It is interesting to note that Orlando Gibbons was one of the late Glenn Gould's favorite composers.
Later in the seventeenth century are the composers John Blow and Henry Purcell.
Purcell's work includes eight keyboard suites as well as his opera, *Dido and Aeneas*.

You might want to compare *The Lord of Salisbury: his Pavin*, by Gibbons with *Pavana: The Earl of Salisbury*, by Byrd.

ITALY. The most famous composer of early keyboard music is Girolamo Frescobaldi. You will find that he uses theme and variations frequently (a topic to be discussed shortly). Try *La Frescobalda*.

Alessandro Scarlatti, the father of the more famous Domenico, also wrote keyboard music.

FRANCE AND GERMANY.
French composers are grouped in the "Clavecin" school. Earlier composers of French music include Jean Henri D'Anglebert, Jacques Champion de Chambonnières, Jean Baptiste Lully. German composers before Bach include Dietrich Buxtehude, Johann Fischer, Johann Jacob Froberger, Johann Pachelbel.

References:
Silbiger, Alexander, ed. Keyboard Music before 1700. New York: Schirmer Books, 1995.

THEME AND VARIATIONS

This form may be new to you; it was not discussed in the *Handbook*, but it is one of the very oldest compositional techniques. Easy to comprehend, it consists of a theme (tune if you prefer, often something of popular or folk origin) which is stated first, then repeated a number of times, each time with a change: different embellishment of the melody, a different accompaniment, rhythmic changes, change of mode, all to showcase the creativity of the composer.

Even before these more formal techniques, there was the ground bass, a bass pattern that was repeated over and over again, with different music for the treble written above it. This led to forms like the chaconne and the passacaglia in the Baroque period, and the chaconne was used by Brahms in the last movement of his fourth symphony.
A precursor of this technique was a simple structure of a bass pattern (not a bass line moving by step) with an implied harmonic pattern. One common pattern was that of *La Folia:*

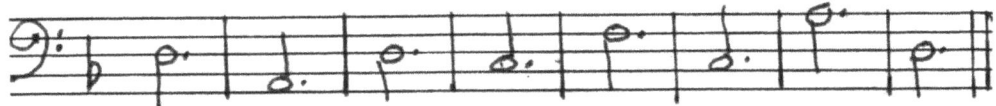

See what you can do with this. First figure out what chords might work, then proceed to embellish them, eventually resulting in a melody. Many composers have used this pattern, among them Corelli.

Even if you see the title "Variations" without the word "theme" such as the "Goldberg Variations" by Bach, there has to be a main theme or starting point before the variations begin. There are many famous compositions using this technique, which will be mentioned in the listings of music.

BACH: the Master
Johann Sebastian Bach (1685-1750)

"A musician's life without Bach is like an actor's life without Shakespeare" to quote Sir Andras Schiff in an article from *The New York Times*, "Exploring the last Bach Frontier, the Piano" (9/12/1999).

Your introduction to Bach was probably material from the *Notebook for Anna Magdalena* (his second wife) followed by some of the short preludes, and then the two-part inventions. Three-part inventions (sometimes called sinfonias) are the next step. If you notice, the two part and three part inventions follow the same pattern of keys in the same order; these are the keys that Bach thought had the best intonation. The three-part invention in E major is a good one to begin with, and don't miss the poignant one in F minor, and the lively ones in F and G major. There is plenty of material to keep you busy, and you should at least read through all of the two-part and three-part inventions, even if you don't complete them all.

If you haven't done any Bach at all, it is advisable to begin at once, with the easiest pieces. Students who have not learned the easier pieces have more difficulty later on.

Before *The Well-Tempered Clavier* could be written, there had to be the development of equal temperament tuning. Those interested in pursuing this subject can look into the following books:
    Isacoff, Stuart, *Temperament, how music became a battleground for the great minds of Western Civilization* (New York, Vintage, 2003)
    Barbour, J. Murray, *Tuning and Temperament, a historical survey* (New York, Dover, 2004)
    Duffin, Ross W., *How Equal Temperament ruined harmony (and why you should care)* (New York, Norton, 2006)

Bach's works are identified by the Schmieder number (the person who did the cataloging), with the letter S or the letters BWV (Bach Werke Verzeichnis). This catalog is arranged by category of works, not chronologically, which was probably the most expedient way, as Bach himself grouped works together (suites, partitas, for example).

Let the Well-Tempered Clavier be your daily bread. More wise advice from R. S.

The Well-Tempered Clavier (should you see "Clavichord" this is a mistranslation), the keystone of the canon of piano literature, consists of two volumes, v. 1 (1722) and v. 2 (1744), one prelude and fugue in each key (24 in each volume) arranged chromatically. Usually the word "volume" is replaced by the word "book". Commentary about each work can be found in F&F and in a small book by Cecil Gray (see references at the end of the chapter).

Preludes have a motif (motive) which is the germ of the musical material from which the work is composed. Your studies of theory and harmony will be of help here. You don't have to analyze every measure, but if you can recognize chords in the arpeggiated figures, hear where the harmony is moving, you will be in good stead. This is contrapuntal writing, but the harmony is always there.

When you first encounter a fugue, it is a good idea to read something about fugues. Get out your copy of Aaron Copland's *What to Listen for in Music*, recommended in the *Handbook*. Here is one of the clearest explanations of how a fugue is composed that I have ever read. Fugues have "parts", usually three or four-part, which means that there are three or four "voices" (musical lines) that will come into play. (Remember the idea of a round, or canon, with different voices entering at different times). The main theme of a fugue is called the *subject*, stated alone, by one of the voices, usually the soprano or alto register, and is then followed by the *answer*, a second voice entering in the key of the dominant, while the first voice continues with new musical material, called the *countersubject*. Then the third voice enters in the tonic key, the fourth in the dominant. The music that follows is termed *episodes*, which spin out the already introduced material through some different keys, and eventually must wind back to the tonic. As there is more compositional freedom here, fugues are usually termed procedures rather than forms. Observing what is going on musically can be a fascinating pursuit. The basic principle was introduced in the two and three part inventions, but is far more complex now.

Where to begin in the WTC, as it is usually termed?

Students are usually assigned a prelude and fugue at their playing level, that is to say, if the prelude is easy enough but the fugue difficult, another set will be chosen. This doesn't stop you from reading through any preludes you'd like. As every key is represented, here is material to help you learn all the keys. People tend to shy away from anything over three sharps and three flats, and this is such a pity.
The first prelude, Book 1, in C, has been overworked (and rearranged!) but still emerges pristine if treated with respect. There are many moods conveyed in the preludes, so you do have a great deal of choice, from athleticism (preludes in C minor, Books 1 and 2, G major, Books 1 and 2) to pastoral (E major, book 1) poignancy (F minor, Book 1) Consider the one in D major, Book 1, B-flat major, Books 1 and 2, A minor, Book 2, has wonderful chromaticism.

Other important keyboard works, from a vast array of repertoire include the six French suites, the six English suites, the six partitas, the *Italian Concerto* (for keyboard alone), the Goldberg *Variations*. It is interesting to note that in the sets of six (Bach must have liked the number six, as many instrumental works have this number), there is most often a balance of major and minor keys. The French suites are the most advisable to begin with here, as they have the shortest number of individual movements. Remember the basic plan of the baroque suite, all dance forms: allemande, courante, sarabande, gigue, and then supplemented with additional dances, such as the bouree, gavotte, minuet. Everyone has favorites; I would suggest no. 1 in D minor, no. 6 in E major. No. 5 in G major is extremely beautiful, but also the most difficult of the group. The English suites and partitas have more movements, and often a prelude at the beginning.

Many students complain about the difficulties of Bach. It is true that with contrapuntal writing, there is no way to "cheat", you either play the lines or you don't. With what might feel like musical "weaving", once you drop a stitch, you find it impossible to get back in, or a good starting point to get back in. Be extra careful about the fingering, and mark the essential finger numbers on the music. The rewards of all this study are immeasurable: you learn how to follow musical lines, for starters.

People with an affinity for playing big chords find themselves quite amazed at the difficulty of playing only two or three lines. Here are some words of comfort from Charles Rosen:
"…Mozart [re Sonata K576], like Bach with his Two-Part Inventions, was evidently under the delusion that two-part counterpoint was easy for amateurs and beginners…" *Beethoven's Piano Sonatas, a short companion.*

When learning a new piece by Bach, work slowly and extremely carefully. Do *not* attempt to learn too much material the first week. For example, in three-part inventions or three-part fugues, work up to, and include the entry of the third voice. This may not seem like much work, but if you learn this much well, it will hold you in good stead for the rest of the work. Continue to work in small sections; it is sometimes difficult to find a good stopping place, but always make sure of the fingering, especially before and after. Sometimes it seems like it is taking weeks longer to learn what you originally thought would take much less time.

A good tip is to review the Bach works that you have already learned, as students have found that a great deal of work is required to relearn them if too much time has elapsed. Try to play some Bach every day. Explore works you haven't played (even the easier pieces). You need good editions of Bach to help you navigate the waters of ornamentation. Bach himself gave a table of ornaments in his *Notebook* for Wilhelm Friedmann. See page 45 on ornamentation for further explanation and more references.

There is an unfortunate trend today to play Bach at the highest possible speed, so long as the performers can whiz through the notes. I have heard recordings of works played so fast that is impossible to "hear" them and identify them if you didn't already know what they are.

"Bach is the most generous of all the great composers, because his works can be played convincingly in many different tempos. In this he is the opposite of Mozart. A good tempo is suggested by the harmonic movement of the piece, and it allows the player to articulate even the smallest note values without haste." Schiff, op. cit.

Bach is the most "adaptable" of composers; yes, some "arrangements" actually work quite well, for instance, those performed by the Empire Brass, and the jazz arrangements by Jacques Loussier. Should you hear a short selection that you really like, find out the larger work that it is from, and proceed.

Despite all this arranging, there are scholarly arguments about whether or not it is "correct" to play Bach on the piano. Sir Andras Schiff advises (in the same article) to play the music on the piano, not get involved in arguments. I agree.

You should become familiar with other works by Bach, such as the six Brandenburg concertos, among his best-known works, and the four orchestral suites. There are many concertos for solo instruments (including keyboard), three sonatas and three suites for unaccompanied violin, the unaccompanied cello suites. There is an absolute wealth of vocal music (Bach was a church composer by profession) so where to begin? There are over 200 cantatas, mainly all religious, though there are a few "secular" (*Coffee Cantata*). You might try Cantata #51 or #80 to begin. There is the beautiful *Magnificat*, which is not very long compared to the masterful *B minor Mass* (don't miss this) or the lengthy *Passions*.

Further reading

An Introduction to the Performance of Bach, 3v., edited by Rosalyn Tureck, has copious notes, as well as the Alfred edition of the WTC, v.1 edited by Willard Palmer, and v.2 edited by Judith Schneider.
Bach, Johann Sebastian. *Notebook for Wilhelm Friedmann* (various editions). Includes a table of ornaments.
Badura-Skoda, Paul. *Interpreting Bach at the Keyboard*. London, Oxford University Press, 1993.
Bodky, Erwin. *The Interpretation of Bach's Keyboard Works*. Cambridge, MA, Harvard University Press, 1960.Much detail regarding instruments, ornaments, tempo, dynamics, articulation, symbolism, and information for a harpsichordist; the author does not encourage the playing of Bach on the piano. See the review by Glenn Gould in *The Glenn Gould Reader*.

Gray, Cecil. *The Forty-Eight Preludes and Fugues of J. S. Bach.* London, Oxford University Press, 1938.
Kirkpatrick, Ralph. *Interpreting Bach's Well Tempered Clavier.* New Haven, Yale University Press, 1984.
Marshall, Robert L., ed. *Eighteenth Century Keyboard Music.* New York, Schirmer Books, 1994.
Newman, William S. *Sonata in the Baroque Era.* 3d ed. New York, Norton, 1972.
Rosen, Charles, *Bach and Handel.* In *Keyboard Music.*

Before we leave Bach, you should know that four of his sons were also composers, but none so famous as their father: Wilhelm Friedmann (1710-1784), Carl Philip Emanuel (1714-1788) who wrote the popular teaching piece *Solfeggietto*, and a text, *Essay on the True Art of Playing Keyboard Instruments,* Johann Christoph (1732-1795), Johann Christian (1735-1782).

"Last, and 'least' of the sons", to quote composer Peter Schickele (1935-) is P.D.Q. Bach (1807-1742?) For some great musical fun, check out PDQ's works, especially *The Short-Tempered Clavier.* The more musical knowledge you have, the more you will enjoy, though many of the laughs are quite immediate, all the pieces display thoroughly musical principles, so there is a lot to be gleaned here.

OTHER BAROQUE MASTERS.

Georg Friedrich Handel (1685-1759) is the other giant of the Baroque era, but he did not leave a great deal of solo keyboard music, mainly the set of eight suites. There is much splendid music to be explored here, and these suites have been neglected most likely because of requirements to learn Bach. The suite in E major, with the set of variations "The Harmonious Blacksmith" is the most well-known. Don't miss Handel's orchestral works, such as the *Water Music* and *Music for the Royal Fireworks*, instrumental concertos. There are a oratorios (you most likely have heard *The Messiah*) and operas, some revived in the twentieth century.

Domenico Scarlatti (1685-1757) wrote over 550 sonatas in binary form (which he called exercises). Many of these should be part of every pianist's education. You'll find practically every technical problem here (possible at the time) crossed hands, scale runs, arpeggios, leaps all over the place, all in all, delightful works. One of Scarlatti's hallmarks is the use of the minor second, the characteristic "bite" which is then resolved. The numbering of Scarlatti's works includes three catalogs: Longo (L), Kirkpatrick (K) and Pestelli (P) one or more of which may be used to identify the works in your particular edition.

Here are some suggestions:
G major (L388, K2) very typical Scarlatti
C minor (L352, K11)
E major (L375, K20)
B-flat major (L46, K47) good hand crossings
D minor (L413, K9) "Pastorale"
A minor (L241, K54)
D minor (L58, K64) "Gavotta", strong rhythm
C major (L358, K95) hand crossings
D major (L465, K96) very typical
A major (L494, K101)
A major (L345, K113)
C major (L104, K159) very typical
C major (L53, K513) "Pastorale"

C major (L457, K132)
F minor (L187, K481) slow
F minor (L118, K466) slow
D major (L463, K430) "Balletto" very well known
E major (L23, K380) "Capriccio"
E minor (L22, K198)
A minor (L429, K175)
E major (L21, K162) Andante-Allegro
A minor (L93, K149)

Scarlatti's sonatas are in binary (two-part) form, the first half usually modulating to the dominant (or relative major, in a minor key). You can observe how this form evolved into the classical sonata form by studying the works of Bach's sons and the early sonatas of Haydn. Check your position at the keyboard if you are having difficulty maneuvering through the arpeggiated lines. Sometimes a small shift of position works wonders.

Further reading: Kirkpatrick, Ralph, *Domenico Scarlatti*. Princeton University Press, 1953.

THE FRENCH BAROQUE (often termed Rococo)

François Couperin (1668-1733) wrote *Pièces de Clavecin*, in four volumes, consisting of suites (termed *ordres* in French, with titled compositions). French composers have always liked to give descriptive titles to their works (a tradition continued by Debussy and Ravel). Couperin also wrote *L'Art de Toucher Le Clavecin* (The Art of Playing the Harpsichord) which will help explain the ornamentation. (for more resources, see the chapter on Ornamentation, p. 43)

A few suggestions for getting acquainted with Couperin:
Book 1: *Papillons, Les Vendangeuses, Les Ondes*
Book 2: *Les Moissonneurs, Les Barricades Mysterieuses, Le Bavolet Flottant*
Book 3: *Les Folies françaises ou Les Dominos, Les Petits Moulins à Vent, Souer Monique*

Book 4: *Les Tambourins, Les Tricoteuses, L'Arlequine*

Jean-Philippe Rameau (1683-1764) also wrote a collection entitled *Pièces de Clavecin*, as well as a treatise on harmony.

Some works to introduce Rameau:
Tambourin (very popular, and maybe in an anthology you own)
Les Niais de Sologne
La Joyeuse
Les Cyclopes
La Triomphante
La Poule
L'Enharmonique

Louis Claude Daquin (1694-1772) also wrote works in a similar style, including the popular *Le Coucou*. You will notice that French composers often use the same subject matter: birds, insects, water, character traits. When you find a piece that you especially like, search out more works of that composer, or other composers of that era. Most pieces were part of suites, so that is a starting point for searching.

ORNAMENTATION

The subject of ornamentation, meaning embellishments of the notes, can become as complicated as you wish, even a lifetime study, but there are some principles to keep in mind, to make things more navigable.

Remember that the main note, the note that is being embellished, is the most important; this basic note is the one you're concerned with, what it's doing and where it's going. Play the phrase without any ornaments at first, to ascertain what is happening musically, and to make sure you learn the rhythm correctly. Trying to work in "grace notes" too soon can lead to rhythmic errors. Soon, you will discover that the music seems "too plain" without being dressed up a bit with ornaments.

Find a reliable source (such as the chart in the Harnsberger dictionary) that shows the symbol for the ornament, and the way it is played (this is called "realization"). You will now have basic information regarding trills, mordents, long and short appoggiaturas, acciaccaturas, and turns. Take careful note of appoggiaturas, and learn to play them in the correct rhythm.

The Baroque era is filled with ornamentation, probably the most of any compositional style. The Classic era also has much ornamentation, probably because the instruments of these times did not have the capacity for larger or sustained sound. Musicians then knew how to play thorough bass and any ornaments that came their way, sometimes they would even "ad lib" and play the passage differently. Music was copied by hand, and different copies often ended up with different ornamentation. (This is another reason to have a reliable edition, such as Henle or Alfred, where explanations of the ornaments are given). Over time, with a study of and listening to many works of these periods, you will develop a sense of what "sounds right". Again, pay attention to your ear.

The "execution" (this is the word normally used) of trills varies from era to era. In the Baroque era, the trills are generally begun on the note above, and likewise in the Classic era, though there are notable exceptions. Playing trills gets easier as fingers are strengthened (see the exercises in Hanon; Mozart even has a trill exercise) but you also want to take note of which fingers give you the effects you want, as there can be some choice here.

For additional study:
The aforementioned chart by J. S. Bach, and book by C. P. E. Bach
Ornamentation, a question and answer manual, by Valery Lloyd-Watts and Carole L. Bigler (Alfred)
A First Harpsichord Book, edited by Igor Kipnis (Oxford University Press)
The Harpsichord Manual, by Margery Halford (Alfred)

Even if you aren't playing the harpsichord, it is useful to read the commentary.
Should you ever get an opportunity to play one, take advantage of it, as well as a chance to play the organ (Schumann advocates playing the organ, if you get the chance, because it makes you hear the music in a different way).

HAYDN: The Mentor
Franz Joseph Haydn (1732-1809)

Haydn shares the nickname "Papa" with Ernest Hemingway. Haydn is known as the Father of the Symphony, but he is actually the father of the classical sonata form as well, which is used in first movements of symphonies, sonatas, concertos, chamber music (such as string quartets). Without Haydn's work, Mozart's and Beethoven's works would not be what they are.

Numbering of Haydn's works was most commonly the Hoboken numbers (H) but newer cataloging uses Robbins Landon numbers (L). Organization of Haydn's keyboard sonatas varies from publisher to publisher (a few works are now considered "spurious" but still might be included; others have been "lost"). This is a very good reason to avoid saying "sonata number" and use the cataloging system number. The exact number of sonatas Haydn composed is not known, because of the missing sonatas, but the number is somewhere over sixty. The main idea is to begin, plunge in, and start learning some sonatas. You may have already played the sonata in C (H35, L48) or in D (H37, L50). There are many attractive sonatas to continue:
G major (H27, L42)
E minor (H34, L53)
D major (H42, L56)
D major (H33, L34)
G major (H40, L54)
A-flat major (H43, L35)
A major (H26, L41) has the *Minuet al Rovescio* (check this out)
F major (H23, L38) is "quintessential" Haydn

For later on:
Don't miss out on the two late and very great sonatas, both in E-flat major (H49, L59) and (H52, L62). These along with the one in C (H50, L60) and D (H51, L61) require maturity of style, so it's far better to learn some of the earlier sonatas first.
Haydn's later sonatas display more of his "trademark" style, especially in the playful themes of the last movements. Haydn's use of minor keys and unusual forays farther afield from the tonic key perhaps inspired his

student, Ludwig van Beethoven. There is also a beautiful work, the *Variations in F minor*, which you also shouldn't miss.

Once you have some familiarity with Haydn, you might go back to his earliest sonatas, and read through them in order. They are a trove of information on how his style develops, and the evolution of both the sonata form and the arrangement of movements within the sonata. The earliest sonatas contain many minuets, and haven't the concept of the fast finale. You will discover that the earlier sonatas use rhythmic patterns (such as triplets) a great deal, and echoing dynamics for repeated phrases. You will also note the use of minor keys (suddenly a new section will be in a minor key). Eventually the standard pattern of first movement (sonata allegro form) slow movement and fast finale will emerge. Haydn's rhythms can be tricky, as an unexpected pattern is worked in, or notes repeated when you think the passage is a straight scale run, but his lines always *flow*. Isolate the tricky bars and work them out separately. Slow movements often require you to double the time in order to figure out the rhythm correctly (e.g., count in eighth notes rather than quarters). Haydn's themes will teach you how to interpret a musical "sentence".

Haydn has a playful sense of humor, which should be observed and brought out in your playing. Definitely listen to as many of his symphonies (they are numbered up to 104) and string quartets as you can, and you will get a better sense and grasp of the articulation, dynamics, and phrasing. Many of the symphonies have nicknames, like "Farewell", "The Philosopher", "Horn Signal", "The Clock", "Military", "Surprise", "Miracle, "Drum Roll". The last twelve symphonies (93-104) are known as the "London" symphonies. The set of six (82-87) is known as the "Paris" symphonies, some of which have nicknames: "The Bear", "The Hen,""La Reine" (take note of the lovely trio in this symphony); no. 92, the "Oxford".

Chamber Music
The string quartets op. 76 and op. 77 are not to be missed (try op. 76 no. 2 and op. 76 no. 5 first).

For further reference (see also the listings under classic period style)
Brown, A. Peter. *Joseph Haydn's Keyboard Music*. Bloomington: Indiana University Press, 1986.
Parrish, Carl. *Haydn and the Piano*. JAMS, vol. 1 no. 3 (1948)

MOZART: The Divine
Wolfgang Amadeus Mozart (1756-1791)

Where to begin? Mozart is one of my personal favorites (it's impossible to single out one composer) so I am trying to convey enthusiasm without going overboard. Mozart is the only composer to have succeeded brilliantly and masterfully in all compositional genres.

There are so many lovely keyboard works to choose from; you have probably played the sonatas in C (K545) and G (K283), possibly the one in B-flat (K570) and you will recognize the "Turkish" rondo from the sonata in A (K331).

Remember that Mozart's works are identified by Köchel numbers, after the catalog by Ludwig Köchel. You may see K.V., which stands for Köchel Verzeichnis.

You should put all of Mozart's piano sonatas on your "to read through" list, just like Haydn's. This is an excellent method for discovering what appeals, finding out what keys the composer used, comparing earlier works with later works, easier with more difficult, the forms of movements, such as theme and variations, rondo, "rondeau" (there is a difference).

Some suggested choices:

To begin, sonatas in D (K311) C (K309), another in C (K330) in A (K331), with the aforementioned Turkish rondo; this sonata begins unusually, with a theme and variations instead of sonata allegro form. K333 in B-flat is a delight to play, and is the only sonata to have a full-length cadenza.

More attractive works include the sonata in F (K332) which has some tricky fingerwork in the last movement; sonata in A minor (K310), one of the only two sonatas in a minor key, requires maturity of interpretation, ditto for the Fantasia (K475) and Sonata (K457) in C minor, forming a set to be performed together, a large work indeed. K284 in D major has a theme and variations for the second movement;

F&F state "it is easy to make a claim for [this movement] as Mozart's finest set". The first movement has some tricky hand crossings. Sonata in F (K533 and K494 is "assembled" from separate movements, and is another large work). The stunning sonata in D (K576) is the most difficult piano sonata. It is never advisable to attempt the most difficult work or works of a composer in your earlier stages; it is far better to become acquainted with a broad range of the composer's work, to get immersed in the style. If you haven't developed sufficient technical facility, the work won't get beyond a certain level, no matter how much you practice it. Mozart has other works for piano besides sonatas (you may have heard of the variations on *Ah, vous dirai-je maman*, otherwise referred to as Twinkle, twinkle, little star.

Some suggestions:
Fantasia in D minor, K397
Rondo in A minor, K511
Adagio in B minor, K540
Minuet in D major, K355
Gigue in G major, K574

A shorter piece by one composer can be a good choice if you are studying a major work by another composer of the same chronological period.

Mozart is considered to be the father of the piano concerto, and eventually you will want to begin your exploration of these (the piano concerto is beyond the scope of this book, but Mozart has 27 concertos, another treasure trove of exploration). There are only two concertos in minor keys (nos. 20 and 24) that some people think are forerunners of Beethoven. It really is too difficult to single out one concerto to start with, but you could choose one from nos. 21 -26 first.

Mozart's other works. You'll want to get acquainted with the symphonies, especially the last three: #39 in E-flat, K543, #40 in G minor, K550, #41 in C, "the Jupiter" K551. Other symphonies not to be missed include #25, K183 "the little G minor",#29 in A, K201, #35 in D K385 "Haffner", #36 K425 in C "Linz", and the "Prague" no. 38 in D, K504.

Don't miss his two stunning masterpieces for clarinet: the clarinet quintet in A, K581, and the clarinet concerto in A, K622. There are many string quartets (the "dissonant", the "Haydn" the "Prussian" sets), trios, quintets, divertimenti, serenades, sonatas for violin and piano, the violin concertos, the horn concertos, the Sinfonia Concertante for violin and viola, the list goes on and on and we haven't even approached the vocal music. Here, the main masterpieces are the *Requiem* K626, his last composition, and the *Mass in C minor*, K427, but there are so many more. Mozart was a master of the theater, and wrote many successful operas. *The Marriage of Figaro* and *Don Giovanni* are not to be missed, and even better if you have a chance to see them on stage.

For further reading:

Schonberg, Harold C., "We're still learning how to play Mozart" NY Times 5/16/76
Henahan, Donal, "How did they play Mozart 200 Years Ago?" NY Times, 7/11/76
Crutchfield, Will, "Performing a la Mozart, whatever that means" NY Times, 7/10/88

These two books are classic references:

Badura-Skoda, Eva and Paul, *Interpreting Mozart on the Keyboard*. London, Barrie and Rockliff, 1962.

Girdlestone, Cuthbert, *Mozart and his Piano Concertos* (reprinted by Dover Publications, 1964)

Eva Badura-Skoda has a chapter on Haydn, Mozart, and their Contemporaries, in the aforementioned *Keyboard Music*.

BEETHOVEN: the pinnacle of human achievement in music
Ludwig van Beethoven (1770-1827)

Ludwig van Beethoven is the musical "giant", and usually "wins" any contest for favorite classical composer, whether from listeners or professional musicians. He bridges the Classic and Romantic periods with three stylistic periods of composition. It is daunting to choose appropriate adjectives for him. Beethoven seems to have suffered tremendously, both in health issues and personal life, possibly more than any other composer. Deafness, for a composer, has to be the ultimate misfortune (you can learn more about how he was affected by reading his *Heiligenstadt Testament*) and to realize what he achieved, often with much work and revision (his notebooks attest to that) leaves one speechless.

Beethoven wrote thirty-two piano sonatas, which form the cornerstone of the canon of piano music, along with Bach's Well-Tempered Clavier. These works provide enough material to explore in depth over a lifetime. Most of us will never be able to play all of them at a performance level (piano superstars will give a series of recitals of all the Beethoven sonatas) but we can always study them, learn the main themes of the most difficult, come back to them years later, rediscover them, and always find something new. In the meantime we will have heard more of Beethoven's orchestral works and chamber music, which will in turn inspire new ideas for the piano sonatas.

Nowadays, the sonatas are often referred to by their order of numbering, which is actually quite unhelpful. The sonatas should be identified by their opus number (Beethoven provided these himself, unlike Haydn and Mozart), so its place in the chronology of Beethoven's works can be easily determined. The "Appassionata" sonata, op. 57, is between the "Eroica" symphony, op. 55, and the Rasoumovsky string quartets op. 59, and you cannot grasp this timeline without the opus number.
"Sonata no. 23" doesn't reveal any information.

What sonatas to learn first? This book assumes you have already learned the two in op. 49, possibly op. 79, and perhaps the first movement of the "Moonlight" op. 27 no. 2. Your teacher may assign a sonata based on what the other students are learning, so as not to have two students working on the same sonata at the same time. If you are planning to audition or enter a contest, you must check the requirements carefully. Some music schools require specific sonatas. For such events, I would recommend *avoiding* any of the popular sonatas, especially those with titles (except for the *Pastorale*). Works that are almost too well known provide the additional difficulty of trying to present them with a fresh viewpoint, and younger students haven't learned enough of the repertoire to deal with that now.

Here are some suggestions for learning sonatas in order of difficulty. Please be aware that some technical issue in a particular sonata might be quite easy for one student, so the student is then learning a work that is more difficult, for instance, if trills, rapid octaves or scale passages, big chords, do not present a problem.

You might begin with op. 90 in E minor (yes, it is a "late" sonata, but an agreeable work in only two movements which is quite "doable"), op. 2 no. 1 in F minor (the opening theme is a "Mannheim rocket") which I didn't know about when I first learned the work; compare with the last movement of Mozart's Symphony K550.

Op. 10 no. 1 in C minor (interesting that these first recommendations are all in minor keys) is truly quintessential Beethoven, displaying the main elements of his early style, and doesn't seem known enough. When Beethoven wrote a set of sonatas (the three in op. 2 are dedicated to his teacher, Haydn) the set of three has two sonatas in major keys and one in minor.

Op. 14, no 1 in E and no. 2 in G fit into this level, as well as op. 31 no. 3 in E-flat.
At this point, you could learn the first movement of the "Moonlight" op. 27 no. 2, or the slow movement of the "Pathetique" op. 13. The other movements are too difficult for this level. I feel it is a waste of time to try to learn a work that is beyond your capacity (it won't "improve" until your technique does) when you could be learning many other works that are less difficult.

The next level includes op. 10 no. 2 in F, op. 2 no. 3 in C, op. 22 in B-flat (a lovely work which Beethoven was said to be fond of), op. 28 in D (the "Pastorale"), op. 26 in A-flat (unusual format, including a theme and variations and a funeral march), then op. 2 no. 2 in A, op. 10 no. 3 in D, op. 31 no. 2 in D minor (the "Tempest"). More difficult are op. 7 in E-flat, , op. 27 no. 1 in E-flat, op. 31 no 1 in G, op. 54 in F, op. 78 in F-sharp. Sonatas with names (publishers' ideas for the most part) are generally very difficult, including the remaining movements of the "Moonlight" and the "Pathetique", the "Appassionata" op. 57 in F minor, the "Waldstein" op. 53 in C (named for the dedicatee), "Les Adieux" op. 81a in E-flat.

The "Hammerklavier" op. 106 in B-flat major is famously daunting, considered Beethoven's most difficult sonata, "the most exacting of all tasks that a pianist can undertake" (F&F) continuing with commentary on the last five sonatas "[these sonatas] present the most profound and subtle interpretative problems encountered in the work of any composer for the pianoforte...There are no compositions which so greatly repay the pianist's lifelong study" (op. 101 in A, op. 109 in E, op. 110 in A-flat, op. 111 in C minor, in addition to the aforementioned op. 106). Op. 111 is even discussed in Thomas Mann's *Doctor Faustus*.
Another very difficult work, a "landmark" work, is the set of variations on a theme by Diabelli. We shall never be at a loss of what to study. Even if we cannot perform these works, they still can be studied and appreciated.

Beethoven's other works: you certainly should start getting acquainted with the symphonies, string quartets and other chamber music, concertos, in fact, as many works as you are able (remember, this is a lifetime journey). The nine symphonies are the gold standard for all composers who follow. You already know a theme from no. 5 and no. 9, and you may be familiar with no. 6. No. 7 in A, is a good one to begin with, followed by a few shorter symphonies: no. 2 in D, no. 4 in B-flat, no. 8 in F, before studying no. 3in E-flat, the Eroica, or no. 9 in D minor.
The sixteen string quartets are the mainstay of the canon of chamber music. By listening to the string quartets, I think you can grasp a great deal of the interpretation of articulation, dynamics, rests, ritardando, more accessible than listening to a symphony. The three quartets, op.

59, referred to as the Rasoumovsky (named for the patron) are a wonderful way to begin; then add the six quartets op. 18. Don't miss the five piano concertos, the violin concerto, the piano trios (especially the "Ghost" and the "Archduke") and the sonatas for piano and violin (Beethoven puts the word "Klavier" first) such as the "Spring" and the "Kreutzer."

For further reading:
Schonberg, Harold C.
    "Did Beethoven ever find a piano that made him happy?" NY Times 5/22/77
    "Mozart, Beethoven and the Fortepiano" NY Times 3/30/80
Holland, Bernard
    "What piano did Beethoven hear in his dreams?" NY Times 8/28/94
Tommasini, Anthony
    "Barenboim's Marathon: a 32 Sonata Test" NY Times 6/9/03

Tovey, Donald Francis. *A Companion to Beethoven's Pianoforte Sonatas*, a bar to bar analysis of all Beethoven's pianoforte sonatas from the first note to the last
London, The Associated Board of the Royal Schools of Music, 1931
Mathews, Denis. *Beethoven Piano Sonatas*. London, BBC Music Guides, 1967
Denis Mathews has a chapter on Beethoven, Schubert, and Brahms in *Keyboard Music*.

Newman, William S. *Performance Practices in Beethoven's Piano Sonatas*. New York, Norton, 1972.
Newman, William S. *Beethoven on Beethoven: playing his piano music his way*. New York, Norton, 1988.

Rosen, Charles. *Beethoven's Piano Sonatas, a short companion*. New Haven and London, Yale University Press, 2002.
Highly recommended. There are chapters on all aspects of piano technique and interpretation of Beethoven's time, and the sonatas are described individually and in detail.

Kullak, Franz, *Beethoven's Piano Playing*, with an essay on the execution of the trill, edited with examples and an introduction by Anton Kuerti, New York, Dover, 2013.

Gordon, Stewart. *Beethoven's 32 Piano Sonatas, a handbook for performers.*
Oxford University Press, 2017. A treasure trove of information. Highly detailed, with thorough formal analysis.

Dr. Gordon has also edited Beethoven's 32 sonatas for Alfred Publications, in four volumes, all with copious notes. The sonatas are also available from Alfred in a reissue of the edition by Artur Schnabel.

REVIEW OF THE CLASSICAL PERIOD STYLE

You will notice a great many rests in this music, whether Haydn, Mozart, or Beethoven, as compared to Bach, who seldom has rests. So many students ignore the rests, as there is nothing sounding "wrong", but the whole idea of what the composer is trying to do disappears, and the piece drags down, losing any buoyancy it would have if the rests were observed.

Steel nib pens were not invented until around 1830, which meant these composers were using quill pens; I can assure you from personal experience that these are difficult to use, and quite a nuisance, so when a composer took the trouble to write a rest (rather than a longer note, far easier to do) he meant it. To quote Charles Rosen (in his book *Beethoven's Piano Sonatas*) "…it was certainly more of a bother for Beethoven to write a quarter note and two quarter rests than to write a dotted half note."

Articulation is extremely important in this style particularly, as the writing demands some "sculpting" so to speak, meaning attention to detail and phrasing. The types of instruments that were available simply didn't have a big sound, and the composers wrote accordingly. No big, lush chords, blending into the next, or a great deal of pedal.

This doesn't mean that we can't play the works on the modern piano, but we should bear in mind *what the composer is trying to say* rather than what the modern piano is capable of producing. The use of *forte* is not the same as a twenty-first century *forte*, nor is a *sforzando.* For dynamics in general, keep the idea of the 18th century instrument in mind, not to recreate the sound, but don't go to extremes. You want to strive for a clear, sparkling sound that is never harsh, and no pounding. Any Alberti bass should be buoyant, as this writing propels the piece along. If your edition has the old staccato markings, remember these are staccato, not marcato. Taper off the ends of phrases, especially at cadences, for a professional sound. "Lean into" the closing chords; the final chord should be a tiny bit softer, unless the ending is a brilliant type.

Trills are generally executed from the upper note, but there are exceptions (your ear should tell you).

Pedaling should be kept to an absolute minimum, if used at all (until you are more proficient with the pedal: see the chapter on pedaling). Be careful of chords in the low bass (again, think about the instrument used then); keep them light, as the modern piano is capable of muddying them (remember the lesson on overtones).

Rhythm is strict. Slowing down, use of the fermata should be observed where indicated. Sometimes you will find a fermata where some ornamentation, or even a mini cadenza, is called for.

Beginnings of works should be scrutinized for the correct rhythm, as many themes are played inaccurately by students, who play the next section with Alberti bass correctly, but fail to count out the half notes in the main theme. An ounce of prevention here: spend the time needed (possibly five minutes) of working out the main theme of every piece you learn, doubling the count if necessary (eighths instead of quarters, for example).

Endings, likewise, should be observed for rests, and for what type of ending it is: an ending that simply stops, with rests to follow (your hands automatically should go up into the air, as these rests are to be observed) or the type of ending with a long chord to fade out (still approached in strict rhythm, no ritardando). Some closings end with a bang, and others very quietly (keep searching for the composer's intent)

For further reading:

Marshall, Robert L. *Eighteenth-Century Keyboard Music*. New York, Schirmer Books, 1994.
Newman, William S. *Sonata in the Classic Era*.3d ed. New York, Norton, 1983.
Rosen, Charles
    The Classical Style, Haydn, Mozart, Beethoven. Expanded edition. New York, W. W. Norton, 1997.
    Sonata Forms. Revised edition. New York, W. W. Norton, 1988.

SCHUBERT: "The Romantic Classic"

Franz Peter Schubert (1797-1828), who lived a tragically short life, even shorter than Mozart's, had been eclipsed in the past because everyone was concentrating on Beethoven. Today, in a global world, Schubert has his champions. His late sonatas are now getting the attention they deserve (major artists are performing the late sonatas of Haydn, Mozart, Beethoven, and Schubert, with various ideas about programming them).

Schubert had a gift for melody, hence he wrote more than six hundred songs (*Lieder*). His piano music consists of sonatas and shorter pieces, such as moments musicaux and impromptus. His style, along with Beethoven's later style, bridges the gap between the classic and romantic periods.

Works by Schubert are generally identified by their Deutsch number (after Otto Deutsch, who cataloged Schubert's works) but you may also see some opus numbers. The main issues regarding Schubert's piano music is it length and level of difficulty; once you are past the German dances, most of his piano works are at a more advanced level; not much could be described as easy. Be prepared for a lot of finger work and reading accidentals.

Two well known piano works are the Moment Musical op. 94 no. 3 (the six shorter works of op. 94 are D780) and the Impromptu op. 90 no. 4 (the Impromptus op. 90 are D899). There are many appealing works in these sets; in the six Moments Musicaux op. 94, don't overlook nos. 4 and 5, but read through all of them eventually. Ditto for the four Impromptus op. 90 (try nos. 2 and 3). There is another set of four Impromptus, op. 142 (D935), especially nos. 2 and 4.

The sonatas have the issue of length as well as technical difficulties. The Sonata in A major, op. 120 (D664) is one of the shortest, easiest, and often performed.
Sonata op. 42 (D845) in A minor was the best known in Schubert's lifetime; there are two more sonatas in A minor op. 164 (D537), and op. 143 (D784), which was said to be a favorite of Robert Schumann.

Eventually you will want to explore all of the sonatas; even if they are too demanding technically, you can play certain themes and sections.

The three last sonatas, all op. posth., are difficult, and have a certain mystique about them (along with the last works of any major composer; perhaps explaining the current vogue for programming the last works of a composer or composers together). Sonata D958 is in C minor, D959 in A major, and the very last, D960, is in B-flat major, is considered Schubert's greatest sonata and has been described as "transcendent" (don't miss this one).

Schubert's other works:
Of more than six hundred Lieder, you may recognize *Death and the Maiden*, *The Erl King*, *The Trout* (used in his *Trout Quintet*). Many lieder are organized in what is known as a song cycle (*Die Schöne Mullerin, Die Winterreise*).

Chamber music: don't miss the two piano trios, op. 99 in B-flat, and op. 100 in E-flat, the string quartet "Death and the Maiden", and the famous *Trout Quintet* for piano and strings (which has a double bass instead of a second violin).

Symphonies: you most likely already recognize the theme from the "Unfinished" (no. 8 in B minor). The earlier symphonies (nos. 1-5) are a good way to begin (try no. 3 in D and no. 5 in B-flat). You don't want to miss no. 9 in C ("The Great"). The numbering of Schubert's symphonies has changed over the years; no. 9 used to be no. 7, but more recent scholarship was the cause of the change.

For further reading:
Rosen, Charles. *The Romantic Generation*. Cambridge, MA, Harvard University Press, 1993. (look in the index under Schubert)

Brendel, Alfred. "Schubert's Last Sonatas." In *Music Sounded Out*. New York, Farrar, Strauss, and Giroux, 1990.

SCHUMANN: the ultimate Romantic

Robert Alexander Schumann (1810-1856) injured his hand, by trying to strengthen it with a device of his own design, hampering his possible career as a pianist, so his wife Clara, one of the first 19th century virtuosos, promoted his piano music. Clara Wieck Schumann (1819-1896) was also a composer, and her music is beginning to be known nowadays. You can read about the love match of Robert and Clara, the difficulties they encountered with her father, and Schumann's mental health problems later in life. There were few composers who ever seemed to have an easy life before the twentieth century. Schumann was influenced by the Romantic movement in literature, specifically the works of Goethe and Schiller. The Romantic movement in music has new harmonies and uses emotion to express its meaning.

Schumann's piano music demonstrates the typical Romantic style and forms: the "character piece" is the most prominent, a descriptive short work, usually with a title that depicts someone or something, a place, even a mood. Nineteenth-century music includes works that are known as "program music", music that describes or tells a story (the program) as opposed to "absolute music" which does not describe anything (sonatas, symphonies, etc.) Harmony now has a wider scope, as well as forms that are expanded.

Most character pieces are composed in sets, often meant to be played completely, and in order. You can discern whether the composer intended the work to be played in its entirety by the last piece in the set, *Waldszenen* and *Kinderszenen* being good examples. Often, selections are simply chosen from the sets. You probably have studied some of the short works in *Album for the Young* and *Kinderszenen*, possibly the *Arabesque or Bunte Blätter.*

Schumann, following Beethoven's lead, gives many of his tempo directions in German, so you will need to look up the meanings (most have more depth in meaning than merely "allegro").

Where to proceed? The selections in *Waldszenen*, op. 82, are lovely (this eventually should be played as a set). Try *Eintritt, Einsame Blumen, Herberge, Vogel als Prophet, Abschied* first.

The *Romanze* in F-sharp major, op. 28 no.2 (good drill in note reading) usually written on three staves looks forbidding at first, but is quite doable once you work the patterns out slowly (remember that not all music is sight-read easily).
Fantasiestücke, op. 12, has several works to try: *Aufschwung*, no. 2, *Warum*, no. 3, *Grillen*, no. 4.

Carnaval, op. 9, is a major work, definitely meant to be played as a whole. There are many short pieces here that you could work on (look up some information on the various characters represented, so that the work will make more sense to you).
Don't miss the third movement of the *Fantasia in C*, op. 17.
The vast repertoire of Schumann's piano works leaves a great deal to be studied. Many works fall into the "difficult" category, so it is advisable to begin with the above suggestions, not the *Symphonic Etudes*.

Schumann's other works include the wonderful Piano Concerto in A minor (which Clara performed), four symphonies (try no. 1, the "Spring") then proceed to the remaining three. The fourth symphony, in D minor, is a major work of the century, nos. 2 and 3 the "Rhenish" are also very good examples of the composer's style and harmony. Don't miss the piano quartet and piano quintet.

For further reading:
Rosen, Charles. *The Romantic Generation.*
Chapter 12 is on Schumann, but there are many more references (check the Index)

Chissell, Joan. *Schumann Piano Music*. London, BBC Music Guides, 1972.

Robert Schumann is the author of *House Rules and Maxims for Young Musicians*, some of which are quoted throughout this book (see page 5). He also was a music critic (you can read these essays also).

CHOPIN: the poet of the piano

Frederic François Chopin (1810-1849) was the son of a French father and Polish mother. Like most of the Romantic poets and composers, he had an all too short life. Chopin wrote almost exclusively for the piano (his orchestral works are for piano and orchestra) except for a cello sonata and some songs. He spent most of his life in France.

There is little of Chopin's work that can be termed "easy" but there are some anthologies of intermediate level works. Once you have studied these, you are ready to try some of the mazurkas, waltzes, polonaises, preludes. Many of Chopin's works are rather long, so it is far better to choose a few shorter works, to get to know his style. To play Chopin well, you must "feel" the emotion, but not overdo. I have read that it requires another "dimension" to make his music effective, as it has an exquisite sound that is difficult to describe. There will be a discussion of rubato and pedaling at the end of the section on Romantic style, necessary to perform Chopin, as well as some other composers of this period.

Preludes. Chopin's *Preludes*, op. 28, are twenty-four in number, in all keys, following Bach's idea, but not his arrangement: these are arranged by the Circle of Fifths, with the relative minor following the major. These pieces vary a great deal in difficulty, and a good number are as difficult as the Etudes. If you have already learned the easiest, nos. 4, 6, 7, and 20, you are ready to do the "Raindrop" no. 15, and nos. 9, 14, and 23. There is also a lovely Prelude in A-flat, not long, which is not part of op. 28, and has no opus number. You can always go through this entire set, playing the first measure or two, to get acquainted.

Mazurkas. You need to pay careful attention to the rhythm in these works, and the correct emphasis (look up the definition). Some are immediately recognizable, and everyone has personal favorites. Here are a few suggestions to get started (take note that most mazurkas are in sets).
Op.7 nos. 1, 2, 3
Op. 33, nos. 3 and 4
Op. 59 no. 3
Op. 63 no. 2

Op. 67, nos. 2, 3, 4
Op. 68, nos. 2, 3, 4

"Nothing in Chopin's whole output contains so much that is original and harmonically daring as do the finest of these characteristic pieces of Polish genius." (F&F)

Waltzes. Some of these have been overexposed, such as the "Minute" op. 64 no. 1, while others do not appear on recital programs often enough. Here are some suggestions: op. 34 no. 2, op. 64 no. 2 (note the "tempo giusto") op. 64 no. 3, op. 69 nos. 1 and 2, op. 70 no. 2.

Nocturnes. You may be acquainted with the nocturnes of John Field, who is considered the first composer of the nocturne for piano (the term "notturno" had been used previously in instrumental works of a different style). Chopin followed Field's lead, and left many beautiful compositions. Op. 9 no. 2 has been overdone, but with new generations of students, will appear fresh. Try Op. 15 no. 3, and op. 55 no. 1 to begin, followed by op. 72, op. 27, nos. 1 and 2. Just as was observed with the preludes, the nocturnes vary greatly in difficulty.

Other works to consider are the *Polonaises* op. 26 no. 1 and op. 40 no. 1 (the "military"), the *Impromptu* in A-flat op. 29, and the easier *Etudes*, op. 10 nos. 3 and 12, and op. 25 no. 1. Chopin's *Etudes* are concert pieces, not exercises for drill.

The *Ballades, Scherzi and Sonatas* are all much longer and much more difficult works, best left for later studies. You can always follow the score and listen to the works, marking down favorites for the future. You don't want to miss out on hearing these works, and you should also listen to the two piano concertos.

Further reading:
Rosen, Charles. *The Romantic Generation*. Three chapters on Chopin.

Other Early Nineteenth Century Masters

Felix Mendelssohn [-Bartholdy] (1809-1847) was a child prodigy like Mozart. His works for piano are many, some quite difficult. You may have played the Children's Pieces, op. 72, and some of the *Songs without Words* (*Lieder ohne Worte*) such as the Venetian gondola pieces. The *Songs without Words* are a good place to continue, with such pieces as no. 9, 23, 45, before trying the appealing no. 1. Be warned that the "Spinning Song" (no. 34) is difficult to bring off. Other well-known (and more difficult) works include the *Andante and Rondo Capriccioso*, op. 14, and the *Scherzo* in E minor, op. 16 no. 2.

Mendelssohn's works include many not to be missed: the stunning Violin Concerto in E minor, the Octet in E-flat op. 20 (for double string quartet, composed when he was 16) is a personal favorite, two piano concertos, symphonies (no. 3 "Scottish" no. 4 "Italian" no. 5 "Reformation," the Hebrides overture and the incidental music to *A Midsummer Night's Dream.*

Franz Liszt (1811-1886) was the first musical superstar, the traveling virtuoso who dazzled audiences with his brilliant technique and memory. (He and Clara Schumann are the first pianists to play their concerts from memory). You will recognize some of the *Hungarian Rhapsodies* and *Liebesträume*. Most of his piano compositions are in the very difficult category, so it's hard to find pieces of moderate difficulty. The "Consolations" are on the easier side. The very difficult works that you might explore for listening include many concert etudes, including the 12 *Transcendental Etudes* and the six *Paganini Etudes*, the *Années de Pèlerinage* (book 1, Switzerland, book 2, Italy) the long Sonata in B minor. He wrote two piano concertos, and coined the term "symphonic poem" for orchestra, writing several works in that genre, most notably *Les Préludes*. He also did a great many transcriptions of works of other composers.

Playing in the Romantic Style

Now there can be more drama and emotion, when called for. Many pieces have descriptions, so it is wise to be well aware of the subject matter and background (such as in Schumann's *Carnaval*). There also might be a personal or literary allusion.

The composers generally do not include pedal markings (if there are some present, they were done by editors) but they assumed that the pedal would be used (see the chapter on Pedaling).

Dynamics can have a larger range now, as the piano of that day had a bigger sound.
Be sure to keep listening for clarity of tone, and bring out the melody, often in the top line. It is easy to get over-enthusiastic and play too loud with too much pedal.

Big chords you cannot reach: this problem now crops up (the keys of the instrument were slightly narrower then): you have a choice of "breaking" the chord, trying to play as many notes as possible in one "go", or quickly jumping to the main notes of the chord. Sometimes the pedal can help. If the chord is totally impossible, you may have to leave a note out. Everyone's reach is different.

Trills in this style generally begin on the note itself.

There is more leeway with tempo and rhythm. Ritardando passages have greater freedom of expression, but always be wary of over-emoting. Take note of the length of the work (shorter works should not have continually changing tempi or surging dynamics).

Tempo rubato: although this did not originate in this era, it becomes the norm for playing Chopin, Field, Liszt, to name a few. The correct way to play a passage in rubato means that "the accompaniment does not vary in tempo. Thus in a true rubato, the melody may be played a bit 'out of time' with the accompaniment, now leading, now following it. In this type of rubato, the hands then, are not played precisely together as the music indicates, but the melody is performed somewhat freely around a steadily moving accompaniment." *The Romantic Era*, an introduction to the piano music.

The other knotty problem is polyrhythms (e.g., two against three). You have come across this before, but with simpler lines. The best advice I have found comes from Ernest Hutcheson (*The Literature of the Piano*). "If…you practice each hand separately, fully up to the tempo required, and then put them together, attending only to the beats where the hands synchronize and letting the other notes take care of themselves, I cheerfully guarantee that you will find little trouble."

For reference:
Dale, Kathleen. *Nineteenth-Century Piano Music, a handbook for pianists.*
London, Oxford University Press, 1954.
Newman, William S. *Sonata since Beethoven.* 2d ed., New York, Norton, 1972.
Rosen, Charles. *The Romantic Generation.* Cambridge, Harvard U. Press, 1995.
Todd, R. Larry, ed. *Nineteenth-Century Piano Music.* New York, Schirmer Books, 1990. (Has chapters by different contributors).

THE PEDAL

Always remember that the pedals are there to enhance the tone, to create a special effect, so to speak, not to be a crutch to connect notes or be a substitute for legato. Basic information has already been covered in the *Handbook*.

Remember that by the nineteenth century, composers assumed you would be using the pedal, and almost never put in any indications for it (a famous exception is the first movement of Beethoven's Moonlight Sonata). Pedal markings were put in by editors. Indeed, it is impossible to play the works of certain composers (such as Chopin or Debussy) without the pedal.

Some pedaling techniques that you will be ready to learn will be discussed below.

Half-pedaling will be especially important for Debussy. A good explanation has been written by Margery Halford in *Debussy, an introduction to his piano music* (a collection published by Alfred):

"After the damper pedal is fully depressed, the foot is moved up and down once or twice, very quickly, just enough to raise the dampers part way. This scrapes the overtones off the top, so to speak, without removing the fundamentals."

(Review the "science lesson" in the *Handbook*, about overtones).

Vibrato pedaling (or flutter pedaling) means your foot is moving rapidly up and down, keeping the pedal in almost continuous motion. This technique is extremely useful in any passages that have rapid changes of harmony, and can even be used to great advantage to enhance the piano tone in works of the classical period, but you have to do it correctly, listening for clarity, and avoiding any blurring.

When you actually want the harmonies to blur a bit, you leave the pedal on, but be vigilant in listening, as this can easily be overdone. For accentuation, you release the pedal quickly.

The middle pedal (sostenuto, but remember some sources will use this term for the tre corde) will sustain a note in the bass while you are playing in the treble, again, infrequently used, but very much needed in certain passages.

Remember that the soft pedal (una corda) not only diminishes the sound, but it also changes the quality of the sound. Learn to use it, but do not use it instead of learning to play in the softer range; use the pedal to increase this range.

References:
Gebhard, Heinrich. *The Art of Pedaling* (1963) reprinted by Dover (2012)
Banowetz, Joseph. *The Pianist's Guide to Pedaling*. Bloomington, Indiana University Press, 1985

BRAHMS: the successor

Johannes Brahms (1833-1897) is the third "B" in the mighty trio that includes Bach and Beethoven: a truly "tough act to follow". Another appellation he is given is the "classic Romantic" (compare with Schubert). Like many of the previous composers' works, much of Brahms is on the difficult side, such as the sonatas and variations. Many of his short works are quite doable. You most likely have played some of the Waltzes, op. 39, which bear re-looking at later on.

His *Fifty-One Exercises* are a must for every pianist, though you won't do all of them, and not in the order of the book. It is a joy to hear exercises that actually sound musical.

The "short pieces" are what you should study at this stage. Brahms has many moods, some exquisitely lyrical (look for the word "teneramente"), others highly exuberant and rhythmic, and some with themes originating in folk music. Some of the technical problems include big chords and reaches, and polyrhythms (see the hints in the chapter about Romantic style). The short works have titles like Intermezzo, Capriccio, Rhapsody; Brahms doesn't use descriptive titles the way Schumann did. Schumann was a mentor to Brahms, and Clara performed many of his works.

Of the short works, the easiest are probably the Intermezzo in A minor, op. 76 no. 7, and the Intermezzo in C major, op.119 no. 3. Don't miss the Intermezzo in A major, op. 116 no. 2. Here are some more suggestions (some pianists are better at complicated rhythms, others at tricky fingerwork, big chords, so these are not listed in order of difficulty): Capriccio in B minor, op. 76 no. 2, Intermezzo in A major, op. 76 no. 6, Capriccio in C major, op. 76 no. 8, Capriccio in G minor op. 116 no. 3, Intermezzo in E major, op. 116 no. 4, Intermezzo in E major, op. 116 no. 6, Capriccio in D minor, op. 116 no. 7, Rhapsody in G minor, op. 79 no. 2, Rhapsody in E-flat, op. 119 no. 4.

There are many other works by Brahms to get acquainted with: four symphonies, no. 1 in C minor, no. 2 in D, no. 3 in F, no. 4 in E minor. (Try no. 3 or no. 2 first). Two piano concertos (the second in B-flat is especially outstanding) a violin concerto, a double concerto for violin and cello, *Variations on a Theme by Haydn* (for orchestra, a beautiful work) and like Mozart, some outstanding works for clarinet (both composers knew excellent clarinetists), two sonatas for clarinet, a trio, and the spectacular clarinet quintet. Brahms's piano quintet is equally stunning, not to be missed, and he wrote three piano quartets as well. There are also violin sonatas and cello sonatas, the horn trio, and the *German Requiem*.

For reference:
Rosen, Charles. *Critical Entertainments*. Cambridge, MA, Harvard University Press, 2000. There are three chapters on Brahms.
Da Fonseca-Wollheim, Corinna, *Brahms's Secret/ He's got Polyrhythm* New York Times 10/21/18.

Other Nineteenth Century Composers for Piano

With all the technical improvements to the piano, the sound and range much expanded, the nineteenth century was indeed the "golden age" of the piano, and practically every home of a certain economic level had a piano, most family members played, so there was a great deal of music being written for piano, not all of the highest quality, by any means. Exercises, teaching pieces, salon music were all composed prolifically.

The fact that so many people played the piano should be encouraging: that it was indeed possible for a great many people to play at a good level of mastery. There were also many arrangements (orchestral reductions) of symphonies, operas, and chamber music for the piano: this was the way you got acquainted with new music, you played it yourself.

The scope of this book does not include great detail on every composer for the piano; there are previously mentioned references that will give almost all-inclusive listings.

Later in the nineteenth century, there were many composers who were part of national "schools" of composition, i.e., they incorporated folk music material into their work.
Listen attentively to all folk songs. These are mines of the most beautiful melodies and will teach you the characteristics of the different nations. R.S.

Spain: the music of Isaac Albeniz (1860-1909) and Enrique Granados (1867-1916) requires a very good sense of rhythm; their music must flow rhythmically without sounding forced or artificial. Albeniz has a major set entitled *Iberia*, and Granados composed many Spanish dances. Manuel de Falla (1876-1946), the third major composer, likewise has works in the Spanish style needing good rhythm. His orchestral works include the piano concerto *Nights in the Gardens of Spain*, the ballets *El amor brujo* (with the well-known *Ritual Fire Dance*), and *The Three-Cornered Hat*, and a concerto for harpsichord and quintet.

Scandinavia: Edvard Grieg (1843-1907) left three volumes of *Lyric Pieces* (don't miss the *Arietta*, op. 12 no. 1). Grieg's piano concerto in A minor is extremely popular, along with the *Peer Gynt* suite. Jean Sibelius (1865-1957) left some piano music, but is mainly famous for his orchestral works such as *Finlandia* and his symphonies (try no. 2 or no. 5 first). Other composers from Scandinavia include Niels Gade (a friend of Schumann) Selim Palmgren, and Christian Sinding.

Russia: there is a group of composers known as "The Five", Modest Mussorgsky, Nicolai Rimsky-Korsakov, Cesar Cui, Alexander Borodin, and Mily Balakirev. There is not a great deal of piano music by these composers, and most of it is extremely difficult (*Islamey*, by Balakirev, for example). Probably the most famous piano work of this group is *Pictures at an Exposition* by Mussorgsky (you probably know this work in the orchestral version, but it was originally written for piano). Some of the pieces in this work are doable at this stage. Mussorgsky also wrote *Night on Bald Mountain*. Rimsky-Korsakov is most famous for his dazzling orchestral works, such as *Scheherazade* and *Capriccio Espagnol*. Peter Tchaikovsky (1840-1893) was not a member of this group, left some piano music (*Album for the Young,* op. 39, the *Seasons*, op. 37) but his most famous works are his Piano Concerto no. 1, the violin concerto, the symphonies, and especially his ballets (*Swan Lake, Sleeping Beauty, The Nutcracker*). Sergei Rachmaninov (1873-1943) is known for his preludes (the famous op. 3 no. 2 is an example) as well as for his piano concertos.

France: César Franck (1822-1890) was born in Belgium, but is usually grouped with French composers. He has some easier piano music (the "short pieces" and French noëls) but his two main works for the piano are much more difficult: the *Prelude, Chorale and Fugue*, and the *Prelude, Aria and Finale*. Franck is much better known for his *Symphony in D minor*, The *Symphonic Variations* for piano and orchestra, the piano quintet, and the brilliant *Sonata in A* for violin and piano.

Gabriel Fauré (1845-1924) wrote a great deal of piano music, but not much could be termed "easy" from the Barcarolles, Impromptus, and Nocturnes. Try his Romance sans paroles, op. 17 no. 3. Students who have heard his lovely *Sicilienne* or *Pavane* immediately want to learn some Fauré, but those works are not typical of his piano music, which requires quite a bit of finger dexterity. He also composed a beautiful Requiem Mass.

America: Edward MacDowell (1861-1908) is the main American composer of this period, and he composed many works for piano. *Hexentanz*, op. 17 no. 2, *Scotch Poem*, op. 31 no. 2, and the *Woodland Sketches*, op. 51 (includes *To a Wild Rose* and *To a Water Lily*) are well known, and suitable for this book's level. There are also *the Sea Pieces, Fireside Tales*, and *New England Idylls*.

IMPRESSIONISM

The stylistic period of Impressionism occurs at about the same time in art and music (in previous eras, some parallels can be found, but nothing that coincides in the manner than this period does). Impressionism has been described as a style that tries to capture the fleeting moment, with the blurring of the lines (in painting and in music), almost a floating effect (take note of the frequent water imagery). I remember an elderly woman at a Monet exhibit, getting too close to a painting, and saying, "It's so blurry."

DEBUSSY: the Impressionist

(Achille-) Claude Debussy (1862-1918) created an exquisitely unique and gorgeous sound, both for orchestra and in his piano music. The pedal is now used for special shimmering effects and to combine harmonies along with unusual scales (pentatonic, and especially the whole tone). He maintains a tonic center, but not in the traditional practice of the past two centuries.

You have probably played some selections from the *Children's Corner Suite* (titles in English because of his daughter's English lessons from an English governess). When Debussy's music was first published, he wanted the titles always to be at the end of the work, not the beginning, but this is not the case nowadays, with the reprints of his music. If you recall music from the French baroque, you will remember that descriptive titles were almost always used. *Clair de lune*, from the *Suite Bergamasque*, is probably his most popular piano work, and often overdone. Possibly you have learned *Rêverie*, one of the two *Arabesques*, or *La plus que lente*.

At this point, you are ready to learn some of the Préludes (two sets, twelve each, for a total of 24, the same as Chopin)
Book 1:
La fille aux cheveux de lin
La cathédrale engloutie
Des pas sur la neige
Danseuses de Delphes
Voiles
Les sons et les parfums tournent dans l'air du soir

Book 2:
Feuilles mortes
Bruyères

More difficult:
(Book 1) *Les collines d'Anacapri*
(Book 2) *Ondine, Feux d'artifice* (considered the most difficult, along with *Ce qu'a vu le vent d'ouest* from Book 1)

Once you have learned a few preludes, you could learn the suite, *Pour le Piano*, or selections from *Estampes* or *Images*, such as *Reflets dans l'eau* (*Images*, book 1) or the more difficult *Jardins sous la pluie* (*Estampes*) or *Poissons d'or* (*Images*, book 2). *L'isle joyeuse* is in this category of difficulty.

Debussy also wrote a set of twelve concert etudes.
Some of his piano music has been orchestrated, so you might hear something that sounds so familiar, but not exactly as you remember it: for example, *L'isle joyeuse* and the *Children's Corner Suite* have been orchestrated.

Playing Debussy's music takes a certain kind of special effort, making sure of the correct notes (many chromatics and an abundance of accidentals) and always listening for the composer's desired effect, whether it is shimmering water, moonlight, wind, snow, fog, a garden, to name a few. Pedaling is of primary importance (see the chapter on pedaling) and constantly listening to and for the pedaling effects. Debussy did not give pedal markings or fingering, so the fingering should be carefully worked out as well as the pedaling. The possible pedal effects and changes provide a situation that has something "new" every time you play the piece. For passages of exacting fingerwork, you must practice these separately to attain mastery over them.

Works not for piano, but that are a "must hear" include *Prélude à l'après-midi d'un faune, La Mer, Nocturnes*, the string quartet.

Further reading:
Schmitz, E. Robert, *The Piano Works of Claude Debussy*. (reprinted by Dover)
A must-have for all serious students of Debussy. Much background and inspiration for the works is covered.
Dawes, Frank. *Debussy Piano Music*. London, BBC Music Guides, 1969.
Demuth, Norman. *French Piano Music*. London, Museum Press, 1959.

Maurice Ravel (1875-1937) was the second famous Impressionist composer. Unfortunately, there is little of Ravel's piano music that is "easy"; if you have attempted the *Pavane pour une infante défunte*, you may have found some awkward passages (and might prefer the transcription for orchestra). You could try the *Minuet on the name of Haydn*. (The idea of basing a musical theme on the letters of someone's name is a time-honored tradition: both Bach and Schumann used this technique).

The suite, *Le Tombeau de Couperin* has some easier movements. In time, you will be able to play it all, including the brilliant toccata. *Jeux d'eau,* a lovely, shimmering work, and the *Sonatine* could be studied once you have attained an early advanced level. *Miroirs*, a set of five pieces, has some easier works. *Alborado del gracioso* is the most famous of the set (especially in the orchestrated version) and is rhythmically exacting. The *Valses nobles et sentimentales* could also be studied, and these also have been orchestrated. (Ravel was extremely adept in orchestration; his version of Mussorgsky's *Pictures at an Exhibition* is the one most frequently used).
Gaspard de la nuit, a set of three pieces, is extremely difficult, best left for "observation" at this point.

Take note of the similarities with Debussy, and the differences: look for references to classic forms, listen for harmonic differences, the use of a biting dissonance, which is always resolved, of course.

Ravel's other works include the overly famous *Boléro*, already discussed in the *Handbook*, plus these not to be missed works: *La Valse*, the Piano Concerto in G and the Concerto for the Left Hand, orchestral suites from *Daphnis and Chloe*, a string quartet, the *Introduction and Allegro* for harp and six instruments.

BARTÓK: the modern master

Béla Bartók (1881-1945) is a twentieth-century master of the piano as well as of orchestra works and chamber music. He is the fourth "B" of the piano masters in this book. Bartók, one of the first ethnomusicologists, spent a great deal of time collecting folk music of his native Hungary, and there is a strong element of folk influence in his works. Remember Schumann's comment on p. 72.

There is piano music at every level, including a piano method (excellent, but not very "easy" as it demands a lot of practice), teaching pieces such as *For Children*, and the extremely worthwhile *Mikrokosmos*, 153 pieces in six volumes (the first four volumes are quite piano student "friendly"). It is extremely rewarding to work through the *Mikrokosmos* diligently, as you will learn a very great deal about music theory, compositional techniques, other scales and modes, forms, and style as well as getting some good technical exercise. Akin to Bach, you will learn to look for the musical lines, and enhance all your music reading and study. These pieces are something I wish I had learned when I was a young student. They are good daily fare for a number of months; then, take a break.

At a level beyond the children's works, you could try some (read through all) of the *Ten Easy Pieces* (*Evening in the Country, Bear Dance, Dawn*), the *Sonatine*, the *Suite*, op. 14, various dances, or some of the bagatelles. The *Allegro Barbaro* is for those who enjoy big chords and boisterous sound.

Don't miss hearing his Piano Concerto no. 3, the Concerto for Orchestra, and once you've heard these a few times, try the *Music for Strings, Percussion and Celeste*, the *Sonata for Two Pianos and Percussion*, and *Contrasts*, for clarinet, violin and piano. There are six string quartets, extremely important in the chamber music literature.

For reference:
Youmans, David, *Bartók for Piano*. Bloomington, Indiana University Press, 1988
Suchoff, Benjamin. *Bartók's Mikrokosmos: genesis, pedagogy, style.* Lanham, MD, Rowman and Littlefield, 2004.

THE TWENTIETH CENTURY

Highly honor the old, but also meet the new with a warm heart. Cherish no prejudice against unknown names. R.S.

There is a great deal of twentieth-century piano music. For detailed lists, check the books on piano literature, and the list below. Here, only a swift overview can be given for the first half of the twentieth century. Composers have been getting away from writing a great deal for piano (especially teaching pieces) and are choosing instead to write for much larger ensembles, indeed expanding on the idea of what constitutes an orchestral work; the same philosophy that is taking place in the art world, as painting has a much smaller place, the large "installations" and multi-media works taking up most of the space. Works for electronic instruments or "prepared" piano are beyond the scope of this book.

There will be much that is new: works without the traditional tonalities, expanded chords and chords not necessarily constructed in thirds, new techniques, such as tone clusters, polytonality, complicated rhythms, including the influence of jazz. Time will tell which works will become the classics of the era.

Reading material:
Burge, David, *Twentieth Century Piano Music*. New York, Schirmer Books, 1990.
Ross, Alex, *The Rest is Noise*. New York, Farrar, Straus and Giroux, 2007.
Tommasini, Anthony. "The Art of Setting the Senses on Edge" NY Times 6/1/14

Music:
Canaday, Alice. *Contemporary Music and the Pianist*; a guidebook of resources and materials. (Alfred) A very helpful and student-friendly guide.
Masters of the Early Contemporary Period, Maurice Hinson, ed. (Alfred)
American Piano Classics, selected by Joseph Smith (Dover)

12 x 11, Piano Music in 20th century America, ed. Hinson (Alfred)
Twentieth Century Piano Classics: Stravinsky, Schoenberg, and Hindemith   (Dover)
Anthology of 20th Century Piano Music, ed. Hinson (Alfred)
The *32 Piano Games* and *24 Piano Inventions* by Ross Lee Finney are an excellent introduction to the styles and techniques, at an easy level.

French piano music of the twentieth century includes the amusing and eccentric pieces (some with detailed directions) by Erik Satie (1866-1925). You probably have heard at least one of the three *Gymnopédies*. *Sports et Divertissements* have understandable titles, while some of his works have titles that border on the absurd.

Jacques Ibert (1890-1962), best known for his orchestral work *Escales*, has a set of piano pieces entitled *Histoires*. Many of the works of Darius Milhaud (1892-1974) have a Brazilian influence. He was a member of Les Six, along with Francis Poulenc (1892-1963) who left a great deal of piano music: try the *Mouvements perpetuels*, the *Trois Pièces*, the *Suite française*. Listen to his Concerto for Two Pianos and his *Gloria*.

Paul Hindemith (1895-1963), a German composer who taught at Yale, left a great deal of that is termed "Gebrauchmusik", music that is "useful" and can be played by amateurs; hence, there are a lot of sonatas for solo instruments, and chamber music. His piano music includes the 1922 Suite, op. 26, *Kleine Klaviermusik* 1929, *Ludus Tonalis*: studies in counterpoint, tonal organization, and piano playing. His orchestral works (listen to these to get a sense of the style) *Nobilissima Visione, Mathis der Maler, Symphonic Metamorphoses on themes of Carl Maria von Weber*.

Russian piano music has much excellent teaching material, and beyond that, excellent piano literature. The preludes of Alexander Scriabin (1872-1915) vary a great deal in difficulty and mood. Some are extremely chromatic (some exploratory searching before choosing a work to study is advised here) and are not easily sight read, because of all the accidentals. Dmitri Kabalevsky (1904-1987) has very enjoyable teaching material, and sonatinas, sonatas, 24 preludes. Aram Khachaturian (1903-1978) also left excellent teaching material, and the well-known Toccata. For orchestra, the *Gayne* (or *Gayane*), which includes the famous *Sabre Dance*, and *Spartacus* suites. Another composer of prolific teaching material is Alexandre Tcherepnin (1899-1977).

Serge Prokofiev (1891-1953), a composer whose works should be heard more often, has music of all levels of difficulty. If you haven't played *Music for Children*, op. 65, read through these pieces. Take a look at the ten pieces, op. 12, *Tales of the Old Grandmother*, op. 31, *Visions fugitives*, op. 22, and always look through the other works in any collection. Take note of his use of the minor second to good effects (Scarlatti used the same interval, in a different way). There are some works that must be categorized as extremely difficult, such as the Toccata and some of the sonatas. Of his piano concertos, don't miss hearing no. 3. His orchestral works include seven symphonies (the "Classical" is lovely, and don't miss no. 5), *Romeo and Juliet*, and of course, *Peter and the Wolf*.

Dmitri Shostakovich (1906-1975) has written two sonatas and twenty-four preludes (composers always seem to write twenty-four, if writing as a set, Bach's influence once again) besides his music for children. His symphonies nos. 1 and 9 are more of an "easier" listening nature, no. 5 well-known but of a somber character. See the reading list at the end of this book for the novel about Shostakovich by Julian Barnes.

Igor Stravinsky (1882-1971) is to the music world what Pablo Picasso (1881-1973) is to the world of art, as both masters had many stylistic periods, dominating the century, and influencing countless others. Stravinsky did not leave much piano music, compared to the rest of his output: four etudes, op. 7 (1908) the *Piano Rag Music* (1919), the neoclassic Sonata (1924) and *Serenade en la* (1925), the three movements from *Petrushka*, plus the elementary teaching pieces. For studying his orchestral works, the ballets *The Firebird, Petrushka*, and *The Rite of Spring* (considered the seminal work of the twentieth century) are not to be missed. If you get a chance to see the actual ballet, the music will make even more sense. *The Fairy's Kiss,* the *Symphony in C*, the *Symphony of Psalms*, the piano concerto (with winds), and the *Dumbarton Oaks Concerto* should also be on your list.

American piano music of the twentieth century shows much influence of jazz in the first half of the century.

Aaron Copland (1900-1990), the author of *What to Listen for in Music*, a book everyone interested in music should own, is the major composer in the United States. His easier piano pieces *include Down a Country Lane, In Evening Air, The Cat and the Mouse. Four Piano Blues* are written in a jazz style. Major (and more difficult) works include a sonata and *Piano Variations*. Copland wrote the ballets *Appalachian Spring, Billy the Kid*, and *Rodeo*; orchestral works include *Fanfare for the Common Man, Quiet City, Lincoln Portrait*, three symphonies, a piano concerto and clarinet concerto.

Scott Joplin (1868-1917) is the originator of the piano rag, a precursor of jazz, and his works have been popular especially since their revival in the 1970s.

George Gershwin (1898-1937) left three piano preludes (with jazz themes) along with the famous *Rhapsody in Blue* and a piano concerto. For sheer enjoyment, try his *Rialto Ripples*. Orchestral music includes *An American in Paris*.

The best known composer from South America is the prolific Brazilian composer Heitor Villa-Lobos (1887-1959). His piano music includes *The Baby's Dolls*, a set that includes the well-known *O Polichinello* (Punch) and a second set, *The Little Animals*, and too many other compositions to be listed here; a good idea would be to get a collection. His other works include the *Bachianas Brasileiras*, especially the one for eight cellos and soprano.

MAKING MUSIC COME ALIVE

What is the composer trying to say?

Try to produce with each composition the effects at which the composer aimed.
You are musical…when you have taken music not only into your fingers but into your heart and head. R.S.

It is entirely possible to play everything (all the technical "requirements") correctly, and still be mechanical, a performance definitely lacking something:"oomph", feeling, heart? We have all heard someone speak in a deadly monotone; you don't want your playing to mimic something like that. Merely reproducing the notes is like translating word by word without any thought to the grammatical structure. What makes a good performance, one with electricity, the notes leaping off the page?

First of all, you need to understand the musical "geography", what key are you in (yes, you do need to know the key signatures, so you are oriented to the tonic key, can follow the modulations, and know where you are…"you are here" on the shopping mall map), in other words, where the piece is "going" (review the chapter in Copland on the "long line"). You need to understand the big picture, the forest for the trees. What mood or effect is the composer describing? *What is the composer trying to say?*

It is far more difficult to play a piece you don't like, and conversely, the ability to learn a difficult piece far above one's abilities speaks volumes. Some performances are enhanced by adrenalin, emotion, mood, concentration; others might be an "off day", a mental block, a "slump". The piece you are learning might not even be particularly typical of the composer (another reason for learning several works by a composer). If the piece is a "war horse", something overly popular and overperformed, it is more of a challenge to bring off such a work.

A great help in learning the composer's style is to study the scores and listen to other works by the same composer: orchestral, vocal, or especially, chamber works. String quartets are excellent because you can hear the individual lines, the articulation, attack, and phrasing much more clearly. Learn to transfer the composer's style from one work to another. Observe the hallmarks of the composer's style. Composers do display a recognizable palette of harmonies and compositional devices that are unique. Above all, keep *listening*.

A teacher once commented that a certain line in a Debussy piece could sound like an oboe. (I was thinking, this is a *piano*, not an oboe) but listening to Debussy's orchestral works really does show you the mood and the shimmering effects being created, and a "voice" breaking through the mist becomes apparent.

To repeat, what is the composer trying to say? This is your connection to the composer, and your chance to convey the musical message.

You must reach the point where you can hear the music from the printed page. R.S.
This might seem a lofty goal, especially if you've never tried to do it before. Try to concentrate on the music bar by bar, without touching the keys.

THE PROFESSIONAL SOUND
We have all heard the recordings of great artists, and perhaps were lucky enough to hear a few of them in person. Their tone is shimmering, sparkling, their pedaling has clarity, the whole work comes to life.
Other than innate talent, how do they do it?

First, by listening. Secondly, by practicing. Thirdly, by understanding the style.
Practicing scales, arpeggios, exercises for finger strength and dexterity (please remember you will notice "progress" by hindsight). No excessive arm motion (this is counter-productive and tiring as well) and good hand position, close to the keys.

Do not try to mimic someone else's playing. You want to achieve your own style and sound. When you have made enough progress in a work, it is all right to listen to an artist's interpretation.

Beginnings are very important: take a minute to get into the mood; think through the first few bars of the work before you begin to play.

No erratic rhythm or tempi (rushing); you must "feel" the beat. Remember there is a natural tendency to speed up when the piece gets louder, and to slow down when the piece gets softer (use this information to your advantage).
Use your performer's "license" with discretion, when allowed, such as with rubato.

No break after a repeat sign (most students will pause here) whether or not the repeat is played.

Phrasing: Iztak Perlman recommends (interview 8/2/11) making up a text for a phrase if the student is having trouble with it.
Taper off a phrase at the close, as appropriate, no ritardando unless indicated.
Think of an artist's paintbrush regarding articulation, degrees of staccato, etc. What kind of brush? Brushstroke? Thick paint or thin?
No holding notes where they shouldn't be held, including Alberti bass.
Keep the piece buoyant when it is supposed to be.
Observe all rests!
Bring out all appropriate lines, with the top note usually emphasized (no heavy thirds, no overpowering accompaniment).
No excessive use of pedal, keep a watchful ear here.

Look at the whole piece (how long is it?) in terms of a dynamic plan; you don't want a bunch of small surges in a one-page piece.

Regarding tempo, there is an unfortunate trend nowadays to play a piece as fast as possible, at a breakneck speed, so that it is unintelligible to anyone who doesn't already know the work. When the notes are flowing so fast that the music is unrecognizable, something is wrong. Tempo is the last consideration. You want to practice slower (when first learning) than the intended final tempo, to aid the muscle memory.

End the work properly, as the composer intended, such as a long fadeout, preceded by a slowing down? An ending in exact rhythm so you literally "hear" the rests?

A review of playing in the correct style is given in a later chapter of this book, as much as already been covered.

Take an unbiased look at the piece, as if you were going to teach it to someone.

WHY DOES A PIECE "FALL APART?
Most likely, you are not being consistent with your fingering, and you are changing it in certain passages.
Have you speeded up the tempo? Even the slightest increase can be disastrous, if the muscle memory is impeded, or you haven't practiced it enough.
Check your posture, hand and arm position, and distance from the keyboard. Some pieces need a little more distance from the keyboard. You might be inadvertently holding your hands a little too far away, making it more difficult to reach certain keys.
Are you tired? Overtired? Music is like math, difficult to do when exhausted.
Can you overpractice? Well, I think is possible, especially if you are reinforcing the wrong patterns or fingering. Sometimes it works better if you let the work "simmer on the back burner" for a few days or weeks, then return to it. You might be surprised at the improvement; if you have practiced earnestly and correctly, it sometimes will take more time for everything to "gel" and come together.

If you have finished your daily musical work and feel tired, do not force yourself to labor further. It is better to rest than to practice without joy or freshness. R.S.
Rest from your musical studies by industriously reading the poets.
Often take exercise out in the open. R.S. Music studies can open doors to art and literature. Some readings are suggested at the end of this book.

You will steadily progress through industry and perseverance. R.S.

Do you seem to be getting nowhere, despite sincere efforts at practicing? Working too long at the same level or plateau without additional progress might mean the work under study is not a good fit for you at this time. Your teacher can judge whether or not this is a "hump" to get over, or the piece should be on reserve for later, while you work on something else.

For further reference
Bacon, Ernst, *Notes on the Piano*. Seattle, University of Washington Press, 1963.
Bruser, Madeline, *The Art of Practicing, making music from the heart*. New York, Three Rivers Press, 1997.
Foldes, Andor, *Keys to the Keyboard*. London, Oxford University Press, 1950.
Newman, William S., *The Pianist's Problems*. New York, Harper and Row, 1974.
Seroff, Victor, *Common Sense in Piano Study*. New York, Crescendo, 1970.

IMPROVING YOUR PLAYING, BUILDING DEXTERITY, TROUBLESHOOTING

Review "How to approach a piece" in the *Handbook*.
Often, progress is assessed by looking backwards, and seeing how far you have come. Sometimes you feel you are on a plateau, and aren't making much progress. Here are some suggestions to move you upwards, assuming that you are already practicing on a regular schedule.

A more intense regimen of scales, arpeggios, and exercises, such as Pischna and some of the Brahms *51 Exercises* (not in order, your teacher will make selections). Scales really have to be practiced, and learned well, for finger strength, flexibility, dexterity, not just to play scale passages. Sometimes it's a good New Year's regime for a few weeks.

More intensive sight reading: here you can spot your weaknesses, such as key signatures, leger lines, accidentals, rhythm, big chords, passage work. What gives you problems? Are you looking at your hands too much and then losing your place or focus of your eyes (this is something your eye physician should assess).

The study of theory, enough to be able to recognize chords and know what key you are in (the key signature is not always the "answer"). This gives you a sense of musical "geography", knowing where you are going, and a sense of the "long line" mentioned before. If you are weak on key signatures, I cannot emphasize enough the importance of writing them out on manuscript paper. Ditto for chords. This is the best way to learn them.

Posture and hand position. Recheck these, as the slightest adjustment may result in a significant improvement. Sit straight, thinking about straightening your spine from the bottom up rather than from the top down. Relax your shoulders under your ears. Your hands may not be as close to the keys as they could be, and your seat might need to be closer or farther away. Watch for any signs of tension, and take a break every 45 minutes to stand and stretch.

What are your goals? Perhaps you want to learn a work of extreme difficulty, and this is not the optimum time: your teacher can most likely find another work by the composer that is equally attractive and more rewarding to work on at this time. Do you absolutely detest something you are assigned? Be honest with your teacher, so a substitution can be made, as long as this isn't a constant recurrence. It is useful to try to figure out "why" you don't like a particular work: is it the style of the composer, or the technical difficulties that are off-putting?

Remember that some pieces do not "read" easily, but with a little work, actually turn out to be easier than you thought. The key here is to slow down and figure out what is going on.

SELF-DISCIPLINE is definitely needed, to force yourself to isolate the hard passage and work on it until you are comfortable with it. Find a good lead-in to the passage, and get a workable fingering that you don't change. For efficiency in learning and to avoid wasting time, this is what to do. This method will take less time than you think; impatience to play the work again from the beginning will result in the easier parts getting much better and the difficult spot will seem even harder to master.

FINGERING TIPS.
Once you have the fingering worked out correctly, don't change it. Changing the fingering is usually the culprit when a piece "falls apart". Follow scale patterns wherever possible. Ditto for arpeggio patterns. For a *sequence* of several similar passages, follow as much a similar fingering pattern as possible (this reinforces the muscle memory). Learn the technique of changing fingers on the same note, not only for repeated notes but also for deft maneuvering. Also know the idea of using the thumb as a pivot, with fingers overlapping.
Sometimes you have to work backwards to figure out the best fingering. Always look at any fingering suggestions in your music; they don't always have to be followed exactly, as everybody's hands are different, but they may have some good ideas. Certain fingerings are standard, others can be altered.

Mark your music (but not too much). I like to circle the fingering for what I find to be an *essential* finger in the passage, e.g., you must have your second finger on this particular note or the passage won't work. You might even have to write a finger number in larger print, or in red pencil.

PROBLEMS WITH NOTE READING.
Make sure you don't need glasses, or a change of prescription. Students of a certain age should invest in "piano glasses" (yes, they really are called that) for the middle distance. People who work at a computer all day also use these. Check the lighting, you may need more light.
For a single note, use the mnemonic devices for the staff; for multiple notes, read up or down, whichever seems clearer (different printings of the same piece may look very different, as sometimes the notes are "squeezed" to fit the measure into the line). Use the notes you know as compass points. If you are still having problems, write the notes out on staff paper. Review your key signatures.
Don't dive into a work without testing the water, look over the whole section or at least the first page. *Should anyone place an unknown composition before you, asking you to play it, first read it over.* R.S.
Accidentals are a <u>red flag</u>: train yourself to look quickly at the entire measure to see if the note in question recurs.
Block form is a method of helping to learn Alberti bass or any type of broken chord; this helps you hear the harmony in a different way.
Are you putting your hands together too soon? Some pieces go together easily, with others, this is not the case. Each hand must know its "part" and have the muscle memory. You probably have experienced muscle memory already: your mind gets distracted and you might even lose your place in the music, but the hands continue automatically for a little while, at least.

RHYTHM and TEMPO.
Pianists often have rhythm problems, as they practice alone, not playing with others. Playing with others (instrumentalists, vocalists, or duets with another pianist) can help. The best way to improve your rhythm is to FEEL the beat, and find a method of counting that you will actually use. Foot or toe-tapping always works well, but some students don't like to do that. Counting aloud works for some. Marking the beats (with

a small vertical line) in a difficult passage can help. Sometimes you have to DOUBLE the time, meaning counting in eighths instead of quarters, if there are complicated patterns. I find this a valuable tip to know.

The study of jazz and pop music will improve your rhythm.

SCALES, CADENCES, ARPEGGIOS

You must practice scales and other finger exercises industriously. There are people, however, who think they may achieve great ends by doing this; up to an advanced age, for many hours daily, they practice mechanical exercises. That is as reasonable as trying to recite the alphabet faster and faster every day. Find a better use for your time.
R.S.

Pianists have to learn scales for a variety of reasons: scales are necessary for building technique, dexterity, flexibility, finger strength. Scales are the source of the keys, so by learning the scales you can learn the key signatures almost automatically, if you pay attention.

Learn the scale *fingerings* very well, observing what fingering pattern the scale follows. The full list is in the *Handbook*, and in many scale books as well. Practice with a firm attack, really pressing into the keys, and work at a slow to moderate speed. Observe where the thumbs fall.

There are twelve major scales (the enharmonic scales increase the number to fifteen, but the fingerings remain the same). You could follow the plan of the Circle of Fifths, by scale fingering families, chromatically, with the relative or tonic minor, just so long as you observe the fingering pattern. Keep reviewing all the scales you have previously learned. Add minor scales that fit the fingering patterns, and keep a record of all the scales you have worked on.

Set a reasonable goal for the year (in twelve months, you could learn all twelve major scales; if you have an entrance exam, double or triple up). Seven minutes a day, if the student is diligent, should bring good results. Check with a timer: a lot can be played in seven minutes.

Begin with two octaves, hands separately, increasing to three octaves, then four.
Try hands together in contrary motion first. Always slow down when combining your hands. Then try hands together in parallel motion, two octaves. Then increase to three. If this isn't working well, go back to

hands separately. Your time might be better spent if you learn four octaves, hands separately, very very well.

Goal: major and minor scales, four octaves, hands together, at a reasonably moderate tempo.

Ask yourself, what is the key signature? What pieces have you learned in this key? Add the key signature to a Circle of Fifths that you keep handy.

Always be aware of the fingering pattern (so many scales have the same or similar one) and don't make extra work for yourself.
Check your hand position; sometimes the slightest adjustment (hand in further) may make quite a difference. Test yourself with hands together, <u>two</u> octaves apart.

Learn the cadences given in your scale book (hands separately at first). What are the primary chords in the key you are working on? Become a keen observer, so you are learning some basic theory..

Arpeggios.
Learn a simpler version first (I suggest broken octaves, through the inversions of the basic triad) before tackling the standard form to be found in the scale books. In some scale books, such as *The Brown Scale Book*, these are included, under "four note form".
For the standard arpeggio, check your left hand fingering, and ask your teacher if a different fingering seems more comfortable and works better for you. Again, practice hands separately at first, paying attention to hand position. Goal: hands together.

If you haven't yet worked on some of the Brahms *51 Exercises*, this might be a good time to begin (your teacher will make suggestions). You might also be ready to try the exercises by Herz (*Scales and Exercises*).

CHRISTMAS CAROLS

Christmas carols are traditional in American and European cultures, so this commentary should work for all musicians, regardless of belief. Musicians play music, and music is a bridge between nations and cultures.
Because of the seasonal aspect, it is advisable to do these studies in the late fall. Hymns and other four-part choral settings can be used during the rest of the year.

Carols are meant to be *sung*; anything you play on the piano is a reduction or an arrangement, but in addition to enjoyment, there are many valuable things to be learned.

Immediate advantages:
Rapid-fire sight reading, so you can hone your skills (carols are short, so you can cover a great many in one session)
Beginnings of score reading (in the four-part arrangements, learning to make adjustments, such as grabbing the tenor line with your right hand)
Drill on key signatures, meters, rhythmic patterns
Learning to make the music "come alive": breathing, phrasing, observing the "long line"
Technique: bringing out the top note, dealing with awkward, unpianistic writing
Opportunities for embellishment and making your own arrangement

Books of carols are often in the traditional four-part harmony, to be sung by soprano, alto, tenor, bass (soloists or chorus, usually a chorus). These vocal lines will use flags for eighth and sixteenth notes, instead of beams, and the stems of the notes will be upwards for soprano and tenor, downwards for alto and bass.
A setting of a carol could be accompaniment only, for a soloist to sing, such as O *Holy Night.*
Carols could have a pop music arrangement, with the chord symbols given.
There are fancier arrangements (such as those by Dan Coates) for piano solo.

Some Christmas music could be an orchestral reduction, such as selections from *The Nutcracker Suite* or Leroy Anderson's *Sleigh Ride*.

Begin with carols you know: see how many you can play immediately, without practicing. For the ones that need some work, observe what obstacles are causing your problem.

Here is a sample lesson, on *Silent Night*.
Play it through, then play it through again, giving your "all" (I have heard this played so mechanically that the effect was distressing)
Where do you instinctively have the urge to crescendo, to use pedal?
How many chords can you identify (there are three: this carol is a beacon of simplicity)
Try to embellish something in the carol, perhaps an arpeggio.

At the end of the season, mark off (in the carol book, or keep a notebook, especially if you have more than one carol book) the ones you've done, and star your special favorites. From year to year, increase your skills and add to your repertoire. Look for places where you can add some variations of your own, which gives you a start in arranging. Observe the texts; with repeated verses, you have the opportunity to change the emphasis.

A few interesting tidbits to note:
Dates of origin, if given
Change of meter in *Fum, Fum, Fum*
Picardy third in the *Coventry Carol*
Modal flavor in the *Coventry Carol, What Child is This, O come, o come Emanuel*
Minor keys are not necessarily "sad": *Fum, Fum, Fum, God Rest Ye Merry, Gentlemen, We Three Kings*
Use of the dominant seventh in a chordal sequence in *We Wish You a Merry Christmas*
Complete scale for the melody of *Joy to the World*
Exercise in thirds in *Deck the Halls*

A note about <u>community service</u>:

Holiday times are sad times for many people, especially those in hospitals or care facilities. Bringing music to them is an easier introduction to public performance, and you might truly be surprised by some enthusiastic audience participation (be aware that some days will be better than others, and be patient). There might be talking, even directly to you. Truly a situation for "playing by ear" in the sense of what you choose to play and the condition of the instrument (you might add a fancier arrangement once you feel comfortable and are warmed up).

If you yourself are distressed at these times, there is nothing better than to get out and do something for others; go and "entertain." (Yes, I'll even use the word entertain.) Bob Hope spent his Christmas holidays for decades entertaining the troops overseas.

You could simply play a selection of carols, or you could bring a friend who sings or plays an instrument. You could even try something you're working on, as an experiment of sorts. The audience will be appreciative and very forgiving.
Suggestion: group carols by key; say three to five carols in one key, so you can make smooth transitions. (Keep a list!) Begin with slower and more "serious" carols, and end with the popular songs.

A few favorite, lesser known carols:
Noël Nouvelet
Masters in this Hall
In the Bleak Midwinter
Once, in Royal David's City
The Boar's Head carol
Carol of the Birds
Ding dong merrily on high
On Christmas Night

Keep increasing your repertoire, keep searching for new material; every year will bring increased enjoyment.

SUMMARY OF POINTERS FOR STYLE

Consider the instruments of the period in which the music was written; most instruments did not have the dynamic range that the modern piano has. Remind yourself of the composer's style in the non-piano works. Make certain your edition is not "over-edited". Often, less is definitely better, in terms of fewer markings.

BAROQUE
Often highly ornamented (look at photos of 17th century churches)
No pedal, except in the rarest of instances
No ritardando
Strict but flowing rhythm
Terraced dynamics in many instances (rather than crescendo-decrescendo)
Balance and clarity of voices in contrapuntal lines; sometimes one is more important; attention to entrances of themes
Careful attention to held notes
Nuances of touch and articulation very important
Observe repeats, no pauses or extra time

CLASSICAL
Clarity and balance of style (look at ancient Greek architecture; Monticello)
Very little pedal; no blurring of scale passages or arpeggiated notes
Texture should be crisp, light, buoyant, especially in Alberti bass
No holding of notes that shouldn't be held
Strict rhythm; no ritardando except where indicated
Careful attention to all rests
Careful attention to the articulation
No pounding or excessive dynamics
Clarity of the themes, with appropriate phrasing, bring out top note of thirds
Let the theme sing out, keep accompaniment lighter
Polish the ends of phrases with gentle pressure, a brief decrease on the final note
Observe repeats generally; the exposition is to be repeated, with no pauses
Careful attention to the ending: what type is it?

The above remarks for these two eras might seem to be leading to a cold, sterile, and mechanical performance; the goal is to listen to the lines, and figure out where the music is going.

ROMANTIC
Look at some European paintings of the time, and works of the English poets
More emotion, dynamics, shading, intensity
More leeway with tempo and rhythm, use of ritardando, rubato
Greater range of dynamics
Much use of the pedal (the composers assume you are using this)
Singing theme above the accompaniment in many works
Clarity, especially in the big chords
If the piece has a title, know what it means
The main concerns are overemoting, blurring the pedal, pounding with too much enthusiasm and too little listening, irregularities of tempo, such as rushing

IMPRESSIONISTIC
Compare with Impressionist paintings
Attention to texture and line
Careful listening needed, especially for pedal effects, sometimes blurring is desired

TWENTIETH CENTURY
Compare with twentieth-century art
The full range of the possibilities of the piano are explored, many new sounds (especially dissonances), non-traditional harmony, and means of articulation, in some cases, literally attacking the notes; even the instrument itself is "prepared" in some way.
Many new techniques introduced, such as clusters and percussive effects.
Influence of jazz
More complicated rhythms
Often the composers give precise instructions and markings, as they have seen what editing can do

The Alfred series of *Introduction to the* (*Baroque, Classic, Romantic*) eras has much useful introductory material.

For reference:
Ferguson, Howard, *Keyboard Interpretation*. New York and London, Oxford University Press, 1975

WORKS REQUIRING MUSICAL MATURITY

The following works are not too taxing technically, but absolutely require maturity to be played effectively

BACH
French suite no. 1 in D minor, Sarabande
Three part invention in F minor

MOZART
Minuet in D major, K355
Adagio in B minor, K540

BEETHOVEN
Bagatelle in B-flat major, op. 119 no. 11

CHOPIN
Mazurka op. 68 no. 2 in A minor

SCHUMANN
Waldszenen, op. 82, *Abschied*
Fantasy, op. 17, third movement

BRAHMS
Intermezzo in A major, op. 118 no. 2

DEBUSSY
Des pas sur la neige from Preludes, book 1

POP AND JAZZ

"When a person...attempts to enter the jazz world from a playing aspect, he often finds himself hamstrung by many varied musical inadequacies...[you must stop to] realize that a jazz technique in many ways is a completely new form of technique when compared with the classical." Oscar Peterson, in the foreword to his jazz exercise book.

How *not* to sound like a "classical" pianist when trying to play popular music?
Unless you can do this naturally, you will need instruction and guidance from a teacher.

The first thing to do is <u>maintain a steady beat</u>, like an "invisible drummer" in the background (tapping your foot, or tapping your toe should work well), then relax with the melody, keeping the principles of rubato in mind. Imagine how somebody would sing the words. Quite a bit of liberty is taken, but a steady beat must be maintained under it. Practicing some jazz exercises can help a great deal.

Unless you can play "by ear" you will need music, and before you can successfully play from "fake books" or lead sheets (only the melody line and chord symbols are given), you need to know your chords. (One of the many reasons for studying theory).

The most efficient way to learn is to select some songs you like and get the music for them (these are "arrangements" for piano, get a copy that has chord symbols). You might start with a musical (the main songs will be in one volume) or a collection such as the "decade" series, Songs from the 30s, 40s (there are volumes for all the decades) or simply collections of "standards". The older the better; the golden age of song writing was in the 1930s era, give or take a few years.

Play the music that is there through first, studying the chords. Then try to embellish, for instance, add an arpeggiated accompaniment, chords in different ranges. You will note that the chord symbols are written above the staff (traditional classic harmonic analysis places the chord notation below) and they are identified as C, C7, etc. If you don't know all the symbols and meanings, get a chord chart and start playing through them and more importantly, writing them out. (See the recommendations given later in this chapter). You need to learn what an added 6th is, as this "dresses up" a plain triad, and some new seventh chords, to get started. More advanced chords can be added gradually: ninths, elevenths, thirteenths.

The next step is to make your very own arrangement. Now you will be doing some real composing. Copy the tune on manuscript paper, leaving room for a piano part, and jot down some ideas. Get the basic chords in there, then look for some chord substitutes and chords that can be added; the harmony will make all the difference. Now you are getting into actual arranging, artistic creativity.

In fact, keep a manuscript notebook handy, right at the piano, so that if you suddenly discover a really good-sounding chord, or chord combination, write it down! These so often unfortunately become "lost chords" unless written down.

If you have a favorite artist whose style you like, see if he or she has a collection of arrangements available; you don't want to copy somebody else's style, but you can glean all sorts of ideas. Some artists are also composers; for instance, Andre Previn has composed jazz solos such as *Like Young* and *Like Blue*.

References:
Manus, Morton, *Piano Chord Dictionary* (Alfred Handy Guide)
Palmer-Hughes, *Popular Chord Dictionary for Piano* (Alfred)
Konowitz, Bert, *Jazz/Rock Course*, adult edition (Alfred)
Peterson, Oscar. *Jazz exercises, minuets, etudes & pieces for piano.* (Hal Leonard)
Excellent studies, and especially good for someone new to the style.
Metis, Frank. *Rhythm Factory for Piano*, 135 contemporary rhythm patterns (Marks/Belwin Mills)
Dick Hyman's Professional Chord Changes and Substitutions for 100 tunes (Ekay Music)
Bower, "Bugs" *Chords and Progressions*, vols.1 and 2 (Charles Calin)
Very useful, and contain exercises
"Bugs" Bower's Today's Chords and how to use them (Nancy Music)
"Bugs" Bower's Today's Way to Play the Standards (Nancy Music)

The following lists of songs follow the philosophy of this book, to get a thorough background of the best material, so the recommendations are from the earlier days. Learning the really good songs first puts you in good stead to evaluate the popular music of today.

<u>Songs of a slower tempo</u> are recommended first. You'll have enough to do regarding the chords without getting into rhythmic problems.

Body and Soul
Over the Rainbow
Summertime
Stormy Weather
Embraceable You
Love Walked In
The Man I Love
Mood Indigo
Someone to Watch over me
Lullaby of the Leaves
You'll Never Walk Alone
If I Loved You
Old Man River
Can't Help Lovin' dat Man
Smile (by Charlie Chaplin)
Moonlight Becomes You
Harlem Nocturne
But Beautiful
It's Been a Long, Long Time
Star Dust
Laura
Night and Day
Smoke Gets in Your Eyes
Angel Eyes
Isn't it Romantic?
My Romance

<u>Waltz tempo</u>:
Falling in Love with Love
It's a Most Unusual Day
The Most Beautiful Girl in the World
Wunderbar
Lover

It's a Grand Night for Singing

Zippier tempo:
Ain't Misbehavin'
Sweet Georgia Brown
Caravan
Satin Doll
Puttin' on the Ritz
Moonglow
On the Sunny Side of the Street
Sophisticated Lady
Tea for Two
A Fine Romance
As Time Goes By
I've got the World on a String
Lullaby of Birdland
It's De-lovely
Tuxedo Junction
It don't mean a thing if it ain't got that swing

Notice the composers' names, and which names keep popping up: George Gershwin, Richard Rodgers, Harold Arlen, Jerome Kern, Duke Ellington, Cole Porter, Jimmy McHugh, Jimmy Van Heusen, Jule Styne, Irving Berlin. Observe the ones you like the best, and the styles you play best, slow ballads, perhaps jazz waltzes.

Some songs are difficult to arrange for solo piano (unless you are a virtuoso) because of rapidly repeated notes constantly in the melody, difficult rhythms on repeated chords, and would sound much better if arranged for the standard trio of piano, bass, and drums. In any case, do listen to Art Tatum's arrangement of *Tea for Two*, both his performance and Oscar Peterson's.

For further reading and reference:
Sheed, Wilfrid, *The House that George Built*, a history of the Golden Age of American popular music. New York, Random House, 2007.
Zinsser, William, *Easy to Remember*, the great American songwriters and their songs. David R. Godine, 2001.

There are many excellent books on jazz, especially those by Leonard Feather and Wynton Marsalis.

Before we leave the realm of the popular, there are certain pieces every musician should know, especially if you are playing in any situation other than a standard recital:
Happy Birthday
The Anniversary Song
The Star Spangled Banner (and all the basic patriotic songs, including those of the armed forces)
Christmas carols, music for other holidays, such as the *Easter Parade*, Irish music for St Patrick's Day
Auld Lang Syne
Ein Feste Burg (all musicians should be familiar with this hymn, as it has been used by many composers in their works)

The Book of World-Famous Music, classical, popular and folk, by James J. Fuld (New York, Dover, 1985) has gone through many editions. There is much information on the origin and history of the famous themes contained in the book.

PLAYING FOR AND WITH OTHERS

Lose no opportunity for making music in company with others. R.S.
This chapter will cover many types of performance, including solos and playing with others (accompaniment and chamber music).

The subject of accompanying brings up the topic of <u>musical scores</u>, of which there are many types:
Your piano music could be termed a score.
Conductor's score, which the conductor of an orchestra uses (this is a full score).
Study scores, miniature scores as well as the larger format, have the full instrumentation, just like the conductor's, but do not include individual parts. Pay attention to the words "study score" when trying to purchase music with parts.
Score and parts: this has parts for the individual players. If there is a piano involved, the piano score will have all the instruments in it.
Orchestral reductions: awkward for piano, but the usual fare for learning [the orchestral part for] concertos and other larger works: these are transcriptions of the orchestral music for the piano, and may also be called a piano reduction.
Vocal score: if the work is a song, it will have the piano accompaniment as the composer wrote it; if it is part of a larger vocal or choral work, such as an opera, the piano part will be an orchestral reduction.

One of the great joys of playing is making music with others, whether playing piano duets, works for two pianos, sonatas for piano and another instrument, chamber music such as trios or quartets, or simply accompanying someone. Sonatas are chamber music, and the pianist is an equal partner, though common sense and courtesy require diplomatic discussions of tempo, dynamics, etc. If a teacher is involved, you will receive more pointers. It takes awhile to get "used" to playing with someone else, and may seem more difficult than you would think, if you have never done this before. With further playing together, you blend the nuances and polish the work together, not merely knowing when to come in. You are partners in music, and this partnership is continually evolving and growing, so that you will be able to "feel" the music together.

You must be faithful to the written notes of the composer, and follow all the rules for style. Orchestral reductions are arrangements, not the composer's actual notes, so there is some leeway here; you can eliminate clunky sounding octaves, or notes beyond reach.

<u>Community Service</u>. Many students must complete a required number of hours of community service, and many adults like to volunteer. A good audience is at a nursing home, as they will be thrilled to see you, and will be uncritical and forgiving, an ideal place for a "dry run" before a recital, for example, and you may find that the feeling of having brightened someone's day leads you to come back again and again. *Know your audience*. R.S.

For repeated performances, you gradually find out which pieces work better, and if you get any "requests". You should be prepared to play "Happy Birthday" because this situation will arise sooner or later. Whether to play "pop" or "classical" is up to you, see what you are comfortable with, and what seems to work well. Refer to the chapter on pop music for hints. For classical, a good collection to start with is *Quiet Classics*, edited by Keith Snell (Kjos).

Use seasonal music where applicable (Christmas, holidays such as St Patrick's Day, patriotic music for patriotic holidays) and have a repertoire of "weather" music, for rainy days, snow days, springtime, autumn, etc. Once you find these songs, write them down in a notebook. You think you will remember them all, but writing things down (and what collection the music is in) is much safer. You may find yourself getting into "gigs": dance classes, wedding receptions, restaurants, parties, and you'll want a ready reference list of music for these occasions.

<u>More formal recitals</u>.
Playing from the printed score. With two or more people performing, printed music is used (with very rare exceptions). Solo piano performances are a moot issue (see the references at the end of this chapter).

Using printed music (the high tech solution of an electronic device prevents this problem, but these are not yet in widespread use) presents the problem of page turning. You can ask a musical friend to turn pages, but often this is not possible, so you have to work out how to turn them yourself (turning ahead of time, memorizing the next bar, even photocopying part of the work). You should rehearse with the page-turner, if you are having one; it is not so simple as it seems, and some people turn the page too soon.

For playing with larger groups (accompanying a chorus, playing the piano parts in a musical, etc.) you of course must watch and heed the conductor.

For serious recitals, it is best to try out the piano beforehand, so you have some idea of the tone and the action. Bear in mind that it will sound much different (and louder) in the empty hall.
This is not always possible, for instance, in auditions. An additional tip for auditions is to read the fine print: will there be sight reading, a theory test, so you aren't caught unaware.
Your teacher will guide you on the preparation, make sure you have the approximate timings of the works (for auditions, recitals, actually any sort of performance) and have an encore prepared.
For a major recital, you need to plan ahead at least a year, maybe even two. Are there specific requirements for this recital? Do you need to follow the "standard" format: an early work, usually Baroque, a classical period sonata, a Romantic work, plus something later, or do you have the option of choosing a theme for your recital, a certain composer, a certain country, a certain time period?
You should always choose works that emphasize your strengths (don't choose the jazzy piece you learned to help your rhythm problems) or a "war horse", which is a well-known piece but overused.

Concert Dress. You should of course follow the standards of where you are performing. For informal situations, always dress neatly and appropriately. For the ladies, SLEEVES, PLEASE! A concert is not an Olympic event, and the audience doesn't need to view musculature. Women string players are even more likely to appear sleeveless, which is totally distracting: the performer looks very chilly in the winter and overheated in the summer. Always rehearse at least once dressed in your concert wear, especially if this is the first time for a tuxedo or a long dress. Make sure you have comfortable shoes.

Memory. Do you memorize almost automatically? It is useful to figure out your techniques for memorization: do you have a so-called photographic memory, where you have memorized the printed pages, even to visualize them with the markings on them? You can try some of the standard suggestions for memory, such as using block form, hands two octaves apart, memorizing in sections.
Anyone who is not planning a concert career in music does not have to memorize. In fact, for most people, the better the memorization, the poorer the sight reading, concert virtuosos being the exception.

The performance. The day before, go over the material slowly, don't overdo. Get a good night's sleep. To insure this, do something to make you tired but not revved up (a teacher once suggested washing the kitchen floor). A certain amount of jumpiness is normal, and the adrenaline may actually improve your performance. Concentrate on the music, not the audience, and stay in the "zone".
When you play, do not concern yourself with who may be listening. R.S. When you are into the performance, you keep going, no matter what. Ignore any mistakes you may have made, stay in the moment. This advice is more than doubly important if you are playing with another musician. Common sense tells you to bend the tempo if necessary, cover any mistakes of the other person as much as possible. Always be gracious and acknowledge applause (practice some bowing at home).

For further reading:
Gordon, Stewart. *Mastering the Art of Performance*, a primer for musicians.
New York, Oxford, 2006

Acocella, Joan, "I can't go on". a review of *Playing Scared*, a history and memoir of stage fright, by Sara Solovitch. The New Yorker, 8/3/15
Henahan, Donal. "Remember when Toscanini Forgot?" NY Times 8/29/88
Tommasini, Anthony. "Playing from memory, the pianist as daredevil." NY Times, 7/7/99

CONTINUING THE JOURNEY: MUSIC FOR A LIFETIME

The ideal is to make music part of your daily life: aim to practice every day (if you think of it as "play" every day, it may sound much better to you) and listen to something every day. Of course this won't be possible every day of the year, but keep it in mind as a goal.

People turn to music, and to the piano, for various reasons, some of which are health-related, for a better academic performance, or clearer thinking. Some of these benefits are definitely understood to be forthcoming, but as of yet not absolutely proven scientifically. What is certainly true is that the person has a better quality of life with some music appreciation.

Those seeking careers in music have many choices nowadays. Not everyone can be a concert artist or a symphony orchestra musician. The piano can be a springboard to the organ (church music), voice, or any other instrument, teaching, accompanying, conducting, composing, and arranging (with very few exceptions, all the famous conductors were pianists first). Further afield are many other professions that involve music: radio announcing, audio technology, music libraries, music criticism, music therapy and occupational therapy to help those challenged with ill health or disabilities. Music students have found jobs playing in all sorts of situations previously mentioned.

Off to college, and not majoring in music? Try to take a course in music appreciation, and you might even be able to take piano lessons for credit. Music majors already have their work cut out for them.

Traveling? If you're away from the piano for a period of time, get back into shape with exercises and scales, Hanon, Pischna, and sight reading. Ease into your regular material slowly, and don't be discouraged if it isn't what it was; give the muscle memory a bit of time. In some cases it might seem magically improved (so students will say, why practice?) Your performance has improved because you have already put in the necessary groundwork.

You may want to "specialize" in a composer you sense an affinity for. Don't do this too soon; you want to keep an open mind. Acquaint yourself with as much piano literature as you can, even works you wouldn't feel confident in attempting to learn: you can always play parts of them. Playing is always the best way to learn a work of music.

COMPOSERS WHO DID NOT WRITE PIANO MUSIC, OR WHO WROTE VERY LITTLE, and not previously mentioned in the text

In your piano studies, you are unlikely to encounter the following composers, who wrote many famous works that you should be familiar with, for a well-rounded musical background. Look up any unfamiliar terms, and something about the composer. These names are listed by stylistic period.

Gabrieli, Andrea. Canzonas and ricercars for brass ensemble.
Corelli, Archangelo. Concerti grossi (try the *Christmas concerto*), trio sonatas
Vivaldi, Antonio. Over 500 concertos; try the *Four Seasons* first.

Berlioz, Hector. *Symphonie fantastique* (start with the second movement). Berlioz is one of the very few composers who did not play the piano; he is considered a master orchestrator.

Opera composers (the whole world of opera is there, waiting for your discovery; try to see a live performance)
Rossini, Gioachino. *The Barber of Seville* (You already know the *William Tell* overture).
Verdi, Giuseppe. *Aida, La Traviata, Otello*. He also wrote a Requiem and a lovely string quartet.
Wagner, Richard. *Tristan and Isolde* (start with the Prelude and the Love Death), *Die Walküre* (from the Ring Cycle). For an exquisite instrumental work, the *Siegfried Idyll*, which was a birthday gift for his wife Cosima.

Dvorák, Antonin. Symphonies nos. 8 and 9 ("From the New World")

Strauss, Richard. *Till Eulenspiegel's Merry Pranks*, waltzes from *Der Rosenkavalier*. Another composer noted for brilliant orchestration. *Also Sprach Zarathustra* has been used in the movies and commercially.

Mahler, Gustav. *Adagietto* from the Symphony no. 5 (then listen to the whole symphony). Other symphonies to try: nos. 1 and 4.

Elgar, Sir Edward. *Enigma Variations*, Concerto for Cello. (You already know *Pomp and Circumstance*)

Sibelius, Jean. Symphonies (try nos. 2 and 5) You probably have heard *Finlandia*.

Britten, Benjamin. *Simple Symphony*. You might have heard *The Young Person's Guide to the Orchestra*.

Vaughan Williams, Ralph. *Fantasia on Greensleeves, Fantasia on a theme by Thomas Tallis, The Lark Ascending*

Schoenberg, Arnold. Before you venture into 12 tone music, try his *Verklärte Nacht.*

SUGGESTIONS FOR READING

The *Handbook* listed some non-fiction titles relating to music. Now you might like to explore some fiction, and your increased musical knowledge will enhance your enjoyment.

Classics

Tolstoy, Leo. *The Kreutzer Sonata*
Cather, Willa. *The Song of the Lark*
Mann, Thomas. *Doctor Faustus*

More recent titles

Barnes, Julian. *The Noise of Time* (2016)
An important book about the composer Shostakovich. Most of the new generations will have no knowledge of this period of history, and what the composer experienced. See the review by Jeremy Denk.

Conroy, Frank. *Body and Soul* (1993)
A wonderful novel that has not gotten the attention it deserves. The Dickensian plot about an aspiring pianist, and descriptions of New York City make for a most enjoyable read, but the best part is that the author consulted with Peter Serkin so all the music information is correct, something that is not often found in fiction.

Mason, Daniel. *The Piano Tuner* (2002) A Joseph Conrad-like adventure, and a favorite of many readers.

Patchett, Ann. *Bel canto* (2001)
Seth, Vikram. *An Equal Music* (1999)
Tremain, Rose, *Music and Silence* (1999)

Some more "food for thought" readings:

Denk, Jeremy. "Every Good Boy Does Fine, a life in piano lessons" The New Yorker, 4/8/13
Jeremy Denk also has a blog, *Think Denk*.

Schweitzer, Vivien. "Wait, you need to suffer some more: musicians often wonder if they are ready for great works" NY Times 1/4/15

Tommasini, Anthony. "Virtuosos becoming a dime a dozen" NY Times 8/14/11

Schonberg, Harold C. *The Lives of the Great Composers*, 3rd edition. New York, Norton, 1997.

Tommasini, Anthony, *The Indispensable Composers*. New York, Penguin, 2018.

FINAL THOUGHTS AND GENERAL SUGGESTIONS

Aim to play every day
Try to listen to music every day, especially live broadcasts (write down title and composer of something you like, keep a notebook)
Every week, review something you have learned, have a sight-reading session, and listen to something new (non-piano music as well)

Keep a musical journal or file of composers, arranged chronologically or alphabetically, with the works you have heard (similar to a birder's life list)
As your listings increase, you will eventually decide on the best format

Check out book sales for printed music
Visit a music library or a music store
Once you know of library resources, you can have your library make intra-loan requests

Attend live performances, including operas and ballets (some events are now shown in movie theaters, although this isn't the same, it is better than not being able to see it). Attend an outdoor concert in the summer and a Christmas concert in the holiday season.
Before you attend a recital or concert, look up something about the composers and the works being played, even better if you can hear the works beforehand

Expand your reading: include something related to music, perhaps a biography of a composer, the composer's letters, literature that influenced a composition
Look for movies with musical themes, and read the book the film is based on, if there is one, or a book about the composer portrayed.

Learn to follow a musical score (start with string quartets before works for full orchestra) look for the scores online that you can print out for free

There is a business page on Facebook for *Handbook for Piano Practice*, where I post a weekly musical tip.

In conclusion, more wise words from Robert Schumann:

Do not judge a composition on first hearing; that which pleases most at first is not always the best. Masters call for study.
The cultivation of the ear is of the greatest importance.
Nothing worthwhile in art can be accomplished without enthusiasm.

and from Wassily Kandinsky, *Concerning the Spiritual in Art*
"Color is the keyboard
the eyes are the hammers
the soul is the piano with many strings
the artist is the hand that plays,
touching one key or another,
purposively, to cause vibrations in the soul"

Recent titles published by William R. Parks www.wrparks.com
Available at Amazon.com or where ever books are sold.

We Remember the Day of President Kennedy's Assassination

Made in America

The Joyful Cook's Guide to Heavenly Greek Cuisine

Boolean Algebra and Switching Circuits

Computer Number Bases

Introduction to Logic

Sets, Numbers and Flowcharts

Beginning Algebra

Handbook for Piano Practice

Piano Practice for the Advancing Student

Colours of Fire

Letters to a Young Math Teacher

Program Your Calculator

A Franciscan Odyssey

Windows to Heaven

Prayers from the Heart

The Nature Watch Collection Book One

The Nature Watch Collection Book Two

Political Economics

The Calico Caterpillar

Animal Tails

Peppin Puffin to the Rescue

Choices

Time to Fly

Jonah the Reluctant Prophet

Earth, God's Garden

www.ingramcontent.com/pod-product-compliance
Lightning Source LLC
Chambersburg PA
CBHW081458040426
42446CB00016B/3299